"A must-have book for every film and television writer! It's an excellent resource on the foundation of any saleable project: a well-developed story. It provides you with a clear landscape of the complete process of writing a professional and marketable treatment!"

— Dr. Richard A. Blum
Author, 4th Ed.
Television and Screen Writing
Professor of Film
University of Central Florida

"For every script writer who's prayed for help to write a great treatment, your prayers have been answered. Halperin's well-crafted book offers up a meticulous — and simple — plan for writing your treatment, from its inception to the final polish."

— Sable Jak
Scr(i)pt Magazine

MICHAEL WIESE PRODUCTIONS
www.mwp.com

Since 1981, Michael Wiese Productions has been dedicated to providing novice and seasoned filmmakers with vital information on all aspects of filmmaking and videomaking. We have published more than 50 books, used in over 500 film schools worldwide.

Our authors are successful industry professionals — they believe that the more knowledge and experience they share with others, the more high-quality films will be made. That's why they spend countless hours writing about the hard stuff: budgeting, financing, directing, marketing, and distribution. Many of our authors, including myself, are often invited to conduct filmmaking seminars around the world.

We truly hope that our publications, seminars, and consulting services will empower you to create enduring films that will last for generations to come.

We're here to help. Let us hear from you.

Sincerely,

Michael Wiese
Publisher, Filmmaker

WRITING
THE KILLER
TREATMENT

Selling Your Story without a Script

by
Michael Halperin

Published by Michael Wiese Productions
11288 Ventura Blvd., Suite 621
Studio City, CA 91604
tel. (818) 379-8799
fax (818) 986-3408
mw@mwp.com
www.mwp.com

Cover Design: Art Hotel
Book Layout: Gina Mansfield

Printed by McNaughton & Gunn, Inc., Saline, Michigan
Manufactured in the United States of America

ISBN 0-941188-40-X

Library of Congress Cataloging-in-Publication Data

Halperin, Michael, 1934–
    Writing the killer treatment: selling your story without a script/ by
    Michael Halperin.
        p. cm.
    ISBN 0-941188-40-X (pbk.)
      1. Treatments (Motion pictures, television, etc.). 2. Motion picture
    authorship. 3. Television authorship. I. Title.

PN1996 .H273 2002
808.2'3--dc21   2001045471

Also written by Michael Halperin

Fiction
Jacob's Rescue (co-author)

Non-Fiction
Writing Great Characters:
The Psychology of Character Development in Screenplays

Writing the Second Act:
Building Conflict and Tension in Your Film Script

TABLE OF CONTENTS

DEDICATION

To Marcia, to whom I am indebted: the best critic any writer ever had. She read every draft and lovingly persuaded me to make each word better than before.

ACKNOWLEDGMENTS

I wish to thank all those who participated in making this book come to fruition.

My gratitude to B. J. Markel for reviewing the manuscript.

Thanks to my friends and colleagues whose interviews made this book very special:

Robert Nelson Jacobs
Lynn Roth
Jon Sherman
Al Rabin

My appreciation to Doreen Braverman, Pamela Wylie, and Lise Anderson and the Writers Guild of America, west, Inc. for their assistance in permitting me to reprint the WGAw booklet "What Every Writer Needs to Know."

FOREWORD

That a screenplay or teleplay ever gets produced is just short of miraculous. Only those who prepare themselves and dedicate themselves to the art of writing will succeed. Perseverance and assertiveness get one through the door. However, once through that door, only talent pays off.

Many talented writers work in film and television, but genius is rare. By studying the craft and understanding the medium, writers can reach their goals.

Writing a screenplay or teleplay is a daunting task. Filling 120 pages with exciting, dramatic, humorous, romantic moments that entrance or thrill an audience can force any would-be writer to reconsider his or her career and become an accountant or doctor, even in these days of managed care and lower expectations.

Neither short stories nor screenplays, treatments "show" with words the story that ends up on a large theater screen or on television. They inform others how well a writer can relate a visual story with all of its twists, turns, and character development. They place on paper the megatheme of the story as well as the subtext before committing to the screenplay.

Treatments also act as a writer's entrée into the world of motion pictures and television. One of the first steps through the door of this highly competitive business may be the sale of a well-developed story. When fundamentals of character, structure, and genre are mastered, they can lead to a successful career as a screenwriter.

ELEMENTS OF THE BOOK

Writing the Killer Treatment takes you through the complete process of developing treatments that sell.

Starting with "A Writer's Map," Chapter One, the book explores the uses of treatments and their value as guides through the methods of storytelling. The chapter also examines the need to research your subject matter.

Chapter Two describes "Exploring Options" by developing believable characters that have substance and shading in order to sustain the story.

"Story Development" in Chapter Three takes you through classic, three-act structure as well as the building blocks that go into constructing a solid story. It also discusses the necessity for decision-making as you progress through the story and the need for foreshadowing and the creation of subtext that will give your story a firm foundation.

Chapters Four, Five, Six, and Seven reveal the story requirements for originals, adaptations, television longform (Movies of the Week, miniseries), one-hour and half-hour episodic television, and daytime serials — the soaps.

Chapter Eight provides the structural underpinning for episodic television specifically.

In "A Final Word," Chapter Nine, each genre is discussed in order to provide a concise review of all the material presented in this book.

At the end of each chapter you will find exercises designed to lead you through the task of writing treatments in a variety of genres. Done with care and diligence, they will give you a head start on the road to creativity.

Several interviews with well-known writers and producers are included in the Appendix. These successful professionals discuss the way they use treatments to develop screenplays for each of their genres.

No amount of "book learning" will do as much for you as sitting down and scribbling on that legal pad or pecking away at that computer keyboard. But that is only the beginning of the process. Then the difficult task of rewriting repeats itself over and over again until what you have on paper reverberates with echoes of superior writing.

Competition is too fierce to consider your work as "good enough." It must be the absolute best you can achieve. Hopefully, this book will assist you in the successful fulfillment of your dreams.

Michael Halperin
January 2002

CHAPTER ONE

A WRITER'S MAP

If you want to write a gruesome horror story, begin with an empty computer screen or a blank piece of paper. That represents a writer's worst nightmare.

In that void sit the fears of every creative individual involved in motion pictures and television — the terror and anguish of filling space with word pictures we hope will make readers or story editors or producers leap from their chairs shouting "Eureka!"

We may snatch ideas out of the air as the result of a passing remark overheard at an airline terminal while waiting to crowd aboard an economy class flight. Perhaps we start with a premise based on an ancient magazine story read while waiting in a doctor's office. An interesting face sipping from a mug at a ubiquitous coffee shop in a local mini-mall might conjure up a few ideas.

All of those triggers mean nothing until they take on the breadth and depth of a real story with a beginning, middle, and end. Those people spotted surreptitiously or bumped into accidentally have to evolve as three-dimensional characters with lives filled with love, fear, ambition, or any one of the seven deadly sins.

An answer to the dilemma resides in a process called "Writing the Treatment." While many writers forced into creating this hybrid between prose and screenplays dislike the form, it does accomplish many worthy goals.

Professional writers use treatments in order to solve problems that erupt during the impulse-driven and artistic fervor driven by the throes of creativity.

Treatments or stories that end up as screenplays or teleplays become no more and no less than valuable instruments in the writer's toolbox. Used appropriately, they can and will assist us in the difficult task of molding breathtaking stories for theatrical and television films, adaptations, television episodes, and even ubiquitous soap operas.

Treatments reflect the intricacies of plot and subtext, conflict and resolution as well as character dynamics. They also present the tone of a story — whether ironic, wry, humorous, melodramatic, romantic, mysterious, or eerie.

Placed in another context, treatments are prose forms of the screenplay without dialogue. They help us to more fully visualize the story rather than rely solely on speech. That isn't to say that dialogue has lesser importance. Certainly no Woody Allen or Albert Brooks film could exist without clever, witty, acid-tinged, neurotic, and sanity-challenged dialogue.

On the other hand, those same motion pictures, from *Sleepers* to *Mother*, have an abundance of semiotics — signs and symbols that communicate everything from a character's motivations to the subtext of the story. Without those visual clues the story would become diminished. After all, we do call the medium *motion pictures*, i.e., pictures that move.

A unique feature of treatments and screenplays becomes immediately apparent: most of them are written in the present tense. Screenplays, no matter in what time period they take place, whether the far past or the distant future, represent the here and now. Therefore screenplays and treatments reflect that creative reality.

SIMPLE STORIES, COMPLEX CHARACTERS

"Simple" does not imply mundane or unintelligent. In this context it means lucid, clear, uncomplicated stories. On the other hand, plots can have major intricacies or twisting lanes down which our characters run.

The greatest motion pictures, plays, novels, and short stories usually have stories that we can describe in one or two brief sentences. Almost all of Shakespeare's plays have the simplest of stories. *King Lear* describes a father brought down by egotism that refuses to recognize true filial love. Overweening ambition leads to the destruction of *Macbeth*.

Relationships between characters make these and other stories compelling. All we have to do is view contemporary classics such as *On the Waterfront*, *Scent of a Woman*, and *Life is Beautiful* to understand the notion of "simple stories, complex characters."

THE "WHAT IF" OF STORYTELLING

The path to creating the story or the treatment can take a number of turns. Some writers prefer beginning with a character and playing with the "what if" moments of the character's life. Perhaps it's based on an item from a newspaper or magazine. Perhaps it's based on an acquaintance. From whatever source the character derives, writers should ask themselves "what if" this person takes the left fork in the road instead of the right. What enigmas will he or she discover? What riddles need solving?

Other times, writers will discover an instigating incident that sets off the imagination. A crime committed, an international event, lost love found, someone or a group battling city hall all have within them seeds of fascinating stories.

I maintain a file of stories culled from newspapers and magazines that may have story ideas embedded within them. If not story ideas, they may hold incidents or scenes that I can use to make a screenplay more authentic in tone and setting.

Several years ago I wrote a screenplay in which a scene takes place in the Cloisters Museum of New York City. I hadn't been to the Cloisters in a long time when I read a story in the *New York Times* that provided a wonderful description of the building, the gardens, and the artwork. I incorporated them into a scene of intrigue.

Stories also arise when existing characters or notions generate the "what if." *Shadow of a Vampire* (2000), written by Stephen Katz, carries the theme of "what if" into surrealistic comedy surrounded by gothic grimness. Katz's notion suggests that the director F. W. Murnau's obsession for dramatic intensity drove him to find a real vampire to play the part of "Count Orlock" in the 1921 classic German silent film *Nosferatu*. The actor, Max Schreck, looks, acts, and grimaces both horrifically and comically in a satire of horror films. Katz has Murnau tell the crew that Schreck is a student of

Stanislavsky and immerses himself in his role day and night — especially at night. Katz destroys Schreck with true vampire folklore: The rising sun kills the monster.

In reality, Schreck continued acting into the era of sound without biting another neck and made his last film, *Donogoo Tonka*, in 1936. However, the audience does not need this information to make the story work. Katz takes reality and walks down the road of supposition in order to create a fable.

RESEARCH AND ROADS

For writers developing an original screenplay — that is, self-generated stories — treatments act as blueprints guiding them through the creative process. Since producers usually want to see completed original screenplays, no one except the writer may ever read the treatment. On the other hand, if a writer receives an assignment, producers may wish to read a treatment as part of the process that includes development of the story through completion of the actual screenplay.

The same holds true for other forms as well. Adaptations especially require, in my estimation, the development of treatments in order to eliminate some notions, expand others, probe characters, and most of all inform the writer if the essential underpinnings of the original material have come through with clarity.

THE TREATMENT AS PROCESS

Writing for television — and that includes everything from miniseries, Movies of the Week, and hour episodics to half-hour sitcoms — usually requires writing treatments as part of traditional contractual requirements.

A reading of the Writers Guild of America Schedule of Minimums (how much producers must pay writers at a minimum) shows the "Story" as the first category in almost every genre. For soaps, the treatment takes another form called the "Long-Term Story Projection." We'll examine that special presentation briefly in this chapter and in detail in Chapter Seven.

In order to understand the use of treatments for television, it's necessary to examine the process through which writers sell their stories. Let's take a hypothetical writer, Ms. George Sand, and the series in which she has an interest, "Indiana," an episodic drama about a dysfunctional family of drifters who live in a fictitious city.

After learning as much about the series as possible through multiple viewing, reading and breaking down several scripts, reading the bible (the background of the characters and plot), and reviewing the stories that the series has completed, the writer prepares several notions to "pitch" to the show.

If Ms. Sand has an agent, she might have the good fortune to "take a meeting." In the event she has no agent, persistent phone calls to the story editor, or the producer, may produce the meeting.

Once inside the door, Ms. Sand pitches her notions. Right away, one of them strikes the producer, story editor, or others on the staff: it has script potential. They ask her to write a story based on her notion. Of course, this doesn't happen without multiple suggestions on how to improve the idea.

Ms. Sand next spends one or two weeks developing the story. In the case of a one-hour primetime network episodic show, the treatment will break into the traditional four acts perhaps with a teaser (a brief scene prior to Act One that sets up the audience) and a tag (a brief scene after the end of Act Four that may summarize the story). For sitcoms, the story breaks into two acts with a possible teaser and tag thrown in.

Upon delivery of the treatment one of three things will occur. Either the producer and/or story editor will like it and Ms. Sand will proceed to a rewrite of the story based on notes or the go-ahead to write the first draft — or they may turn thumbs down and that ends the process.

The treatment plays an important part because producers and story editors can use it to judge the quality of writing, the ability of Ms. Sand to understand their show, deliver on time, and whether or not she fits into "Indiana's" creative jigsaw puzzle.

The same procedure takes place with longform television as well. Although the producers probably hired Ms. Sand to develop the story because of her reputation and ability, they may wish to view a treatment in order to avoid future problems and pitfalls in the story or with production and casting. As with feature films, the treatment becomes the tool that identifies potential difficulties, including some of the more obvious holes in story and plot that can destroy good storytelling.

One of the questions often asked is, "How long should a treatment be?" To use an ancient comeback for such a query, "How long is a piece of string?" It all depends. It depends on the writer, the story, and how much detail the writer and the producers wish to include.

Treatments that writers use for themselves for original theatrical features and original films for cable may range from one or two pages to those that almost approximate the length of a finished screenplay. One screenwriter wrote a story for a successful film that ran over 90 pages. After that, writing the screenplay became a process of including the dialogue with the action.

Writing a treatment doesn't mean changes will not take place. Of course they do. Writing is a dynamic process. Anyone who links him or herself so firmly to the treatment that the script can not take off in other directions does a disservice to the innate vitality required to create characters and stories that intrigue audiences.

Miniseries, Movies of the Week, and episodic television that play on commercial stations have a fairly standard length. A Movie of the Week (two hours) consists of seven acts. Each act has approximately 5-8 scenes per act. The treatment reflects the act with approximately 3-5 pages per act. Multiply that number by the broadcast length of the project. Therefore a treatment for a two-hour MOW might have approximately 21-35 pages single-spaced or 35-50 pages double-spaced typed in 12 point Courier.

A one-hour primetime network episodic television script such as *ER*, *The West Wing*, *Law & Order*, or *Ally McBeal* has four acts. Again each act has approximately 5-8 scenes. Therefore the treatment or story runs approximately 12-20 pages single-spaced.

Never consider any of these numbers and lengths as hard and fast rules. Every project is unique.

For example, I wrote a story and teleplay for the one-hour

episodic television series *Falcon Crest*. Classified as a primetime soap, it took place in a fictional version of the Napa Valley of California.

The first script I did for the series in its first season was called "House of Cards." My treatment typed double-space ran 37 pages. The first act consisted of 10 scenes in 7 pages. Act One of the first draft teleplay had 9 scenes in 19 pages. That sounds a bit long, but the series tended to be dialogue heavy.

For another episode of the same series I wrote the treatment single-spaced and it ran 18 pages. The first act alone consisted of 12 scenes in 5 pages. In this case, the treatment translated into the final teleplay with very few changes.

On the other hand, my first draft treatment for an episode of *Star Trek: The Next Generation* ran a total of 12 double-spaced pages including a Teaser and a Tag. Due to additional commercial breaks as a syndicated series, *ST:TNG* had five acts. The initial scene breakdowns in my treatment were Teaser, Act 1: 6 scenes, Act 2: 5 scenes, Act 3: 6 scenes, Act 4: 4 scenes, Act 5: 4 scenes, Tag.

I raise these examples to demonstrate that no hard and fast rules exist in treatment or story development. Often, producers or story editors determine what kind of treatments they want. Some dislike lengthy descriptions. Others want a carefully detailed explication of the story, characters, and their interactions. It's important to know the show and its idiosyncrasies.

The daytime soap is another beast altogether. Due to their five-day-a-week regimen, their multitude of story lines, and their large cast of characters, soaps work off of long-term projections.

A projection will take story lines out over a six- to twelve-month span. The objective has to do with maintaining logic (at least the logic that the series sets up) over a long period of time and numerous daily episodes.

A number of years ago, I wrote a six-month projection for the CBS daytime soap *Capitol*. The series dealt with a political family and its life and intrigues in Washington, D.C.

The six-month projection ran 96 pages and covered 14 main characters plus subsidiary characters. The stories intertwined in order to maintain the ongoing relationships. My task was to take the characters and their stories and raise them up a few notches in order to create additional excitement as well as provide springboards for continuing action beyond the projection.

SUMMING UP

Developing the treatment becomes an exercise in creative discipline. Without a guide, writers often find themselves faced with the infamous "writer's block." That syndrome usually indicates that no plan exists for continuing the story beyond the initial flush of excitement over an idea that may have had excellent possibilities.

Treatments also have utility in discovering weaknesses in story, plot, and character development before creating the actual screenplay. While it may seem an unnecessary step in the rush toward developing your brilliant idea, you may find that writing a treatment spurs your imagination more than it slows it down.

With experience you may discover that you can take shortcuts. You may not have to write a full treatment after your fifth or sixth screenplay. You may only need to develop a step outline or beats to keep you going.

Don't take short cuts to the shortcut. Begin with the treatment or story until you become comfortable with the process. No one ever succeeded without paying attention to detail, structure, proper story development, and character development. The treatment helps you enter that comfort zone.

EXERCISES

Choose a character from a motion picture.

A. Describe the choices the character makes at the moment of the instigating incident.

B. Outline the story as if the character chose a different path.

CHAPTER TWO

EXPLORING OPTIONS

"Do characters or story come first?" That question always arises during any discussion of the writing process.

Similar to the question about treatment length, the answer *depends*. It depends on what triggers the need to sit down and spend weeks or perhaps months writing 120 pages.

Steve Martin discussed the first inkling of what became a seed that sprouted into his screenplay *Bowfinger* (1999). "I was thinking of when I was 19 years old and came to Hollywood and didn't know what to do. The moment in the movie that's the closest to my actual experience is when Heather Graham gets off the bus and says, 'Where do I go to be an actress?'"[1]

However, the notion or initial idea means nothing without execution. Execution depends mainly on who populates the story. In the case of *Bowfinger*, Martin began with someone who was not the principal character. The idea of the naive, ambitious wannabe becomes the symbol for Bowfinger's skewed drive for success as well as everyone else's Tinseltown dreams and fantasies.

---

[1] Annie Nocenti, "Writing Bowfinger: A Talk with Steve Martin," *Scenario: The Magazine of Screenwriting Art*, Vol. 5, No. 3, 56.

Ideas can also pop up when least expected. Christopher McQuarrie, who wrote the original screenplay that won the 1996 Academy Award for *The Usual Suspects*, had his inspiration when he "was reading an article headlined 'The Usual Suspects,' and I thought that would be a cool title for a movie, what would it be about? It would be about the guys who were always brought in by the police when there was a crime. I could see the poster — there'd be five or seven of them in a lineup."[2]

It's important to keep our eyes open and continually take advantage of opportunities that surround us. In both of these films — *Bowfinger* and *The Usual Suspects* — writers began with fascinating and interesting characters who could grab our attention.

CHARACTER DEVELOPMENT

A treatment provides us with one of the best means for creating meaningful characters. Before thinking about dialogue and before considering the way a character looks, we ought to examine the lives of our main characters. Not only should we consider who and what they are during the life of the screenplay, but also understand where they came from before the first frame and where they may end up long after end credits roll on the screen.

That may seem odd, especially when viewing films such as *Being John Malkovich* (1999) or even *X-Men* (2000). However, if you examine the characters and the way they act and react, their motivations have their own logic. Each aspect of the biography briefly explores the strengths, weaknesses, talents, and intellect of the characters.

---

[2] Jamie Malinowski, "Shaping Words Into an Oscar: Six Writers Who Did," *New York Times*, March 18, 2001.

For *Being John Malkovich*, the writer, Charlie Kaufman, had a vision of his main character, the puppeteer Craig Schwartz. "...Craig is lonely in this world and he's got this very romantic idea that requires other people be puppets for him and do his bidding. He wants that from Maxine. In his mind, if Maxine were to be like the puppet Maxine, he would become this graceful person in the world. He would be able to be this guy he can't be with his wife. He hates that he can't be that way with his wife. That's the sad part of it, they don't connect. He clearly doesn't see his wife. I'm not sure she sees him, either."[3]

Kaufman and other writers may create strange, skewed, odd worlds, but they also create those worlds with their own rules. One of the many reasons *Malkovich* works has to do with those rules. Once we accept the notion that a group of people use strange portals as a method for staying young, then the portal into John Malkovich takes on its own sense of logic.

The other part of Kaufman's story has to do with Craig's life that he sees as one disappointment after another. His fantasy becomes reality and he can free himself from the sordid world in which he lives.

Another thread in the story revolves around a gender-bending issue. The story posits that every person has a touch of the other sex within him or her. The writer explores how characters can use that other side as a way toward self-discovery.

Each aspect of the story comes as a surprise. And while the surprises give us a jolt, they work within the rules that Kaufman set up from the very beginning of the story.

---

[3] Annie Nocenti, "Writing *Being John Malcovich*: A Talk with Charlie Kaufman," *Scenario: The Magazine of Screenwriting Art*, Vol. 5, No. 3, 102.

Whether or not he prepared a written biography of his main characters, he does know what makes them tick. For those of us who require more finite information before plunging into the writing process, preparing the biography can provide the key that opens the door to understanding character motivation. We don't have to make it lengthy, but it should provide us with sufficient information to help us understand why characters act and react the way they do.

CREATING THE BIOGRAPHY

Let's take a look at the contents of a typical biography. We should know the characters' families of origin. Do they have mothers and fathers or do they come from single-parent homes? Perhaps the characters became orphaned at an early age and strangers reared them.

Anne of Green Gables, from the novels by Lucy Maud Armstrong produced as three miniseries (1985, 1987, 2000), written by Kevin Sullivan (Laurie Pearson co-wrote the last sequel in 2000) for public television, has its basis in a single-minded orphaned girl living in the Maritime Provinces of Canada.

Anne has to face a constant battle with children who come from intact families. Shored up by her adopted family, she becomes a determined young woman intent on making a success out of her life. In *Anne of Green Gables*, the protagonist creates surrogate siblings out of her friends.

When developing the character biography, examine the relationships with siblings if they exist. The biography helps inform us how characters connect with other people.

What kind of education do characters have? Understanding the educational underpinnings can provide us with an attitude for the characters to express.

For example, in the film *Scent of a Woman* (1992) written by Bo Goldman, a young student, Charlie, comes from a blue-collar family and attends a prestigious prep school on a scholarship. His nemesis at school, George, has moneyed parents and thinks nothing of humiliating Charlie whenever possible because he considers him from a lower socioeconomic stratum. The prep school provides the environment in which both live. However, they view it from two different perspectives. Charlie sees it as a privilege to attend the school. George adopts an attitude that his place in school comes from an ordained right. Those insights set the stage for the manner in which Charlie reacts to the world around him and the situations in which he finds himself.

Another facet to examine in the biography involves traumas in our characters' lives. Usually these existential shocks surround major life events: birth, marriage, divorce, death, illness, and war, among others. They color characters' lives by upsetting the balance of life. In good storytelling, traumas push characters onto roads least expected.

With *American Beauty* (1999), written by Alan Ball, the character of Lester Burnham faces a deep mid-life crisis — a key existential crisis in both male and female lives. Caged in what he considers a fruitless job and involved in a marriage gone sour with children who either ignore him or consider him irrelevant, he sees life ending without meaning. He wants to revivify himself with false hopes and false images revolving around one of his daughter's friends, a nubile adolescent about whom he has sexual fantasies.

Lester's dream life becomes partial reality leading to a downward spiral toward inevitable disaster. The disaster, as with many good stories, involves the trauma of ordinary life when secrets, hidden not only from others but also from the characters, reveal themselves with dramatic irony.

While all of this may seem onerous, the biography should not exceed one page and go no farther than the moment where our story begins. In addition, not all of the information we place in the life of our characters has to find itself in the story. However, as creators we ought to know much more about the characters than we utilize. That provides us with the knowledge necessary to write strong, three-dimensional characters who have an impact on audiences.

Keep in mind, however, that we have not carved the biography — and for that matter, the treatment and the screenplay — in stone as an eternal, unchanging document. All creative endeavors have rhythms that ebb and flow as they progress. Characters take on lives of their own, permitting stories to rush down unforeseen paths leading us toward ever more interesting landscapes. When that occurs, we should prepare ourselves to rewrite the biography so that it reflects new understandings about our characters.

When I wrote the story for the *Star Trek: The Next Generation* episode of "Lonely Among Us," I received a large packet of materials that included a bio on Capt. Jean-Luc Picard written by the series creator Gene Roddenberry. It encompassed many of the details discussed above.

Roddenberry's biography of Picard mentions that he was born in Paris, France. He "...has his share of idiosyncrasies, one being the fact he is not fully comfortable with having <u>families</u> <u>and</u> <u>children</u> aboard a vessel he commands." In addition, Roddenberry describes Picard as "…still young by 24th century standards, he has gone the way we saw Kirk going, content with 'starship love,' a personal attribute accentuated by his long, long U.S.S. Stargazer duty. But here on the Enterprise, with over a thousand crewpersons and family members, he is also learning that life is more complex than he ever imagined." [4]

By the third season of the series, Roddenberry had rewritten a portion of Picard's biography to reflect changes in the direction of the character. Picard becomes "distinguished," perhaps reflecting the personality of the actor who portrayed him, Patrick Stewart. He also becomes more authoritarian because Roddenberry writes that "Picard demands absolute authority in his role as Starship Captain." [5] He also enjoys "the eccentricities permitted" because of his privileged rank, including making "his prejudices known to his crew." Those added aspects of Picard's character move a long way toward making him more human. They also furnish writers with additional ammunition in developing stories built around character traits.

We should not see change as an enemy. It can give us a better handle on our characters whether we create them for a self-contained motion picture or for an ongoing series.

---

[4] Gene Roddenberry, "Writer/Direcor's Guide," *Star Trek: The Next Generation*, March 23, 1987, 23.
[5] Gene Roddenberry, "Writers'/Directors' Guide '89-'90," *Star Trek: The Next Generation*, Aug. 1989, 7.

SUMMING UP

Although treatments are blueprints for the script containing most of the elements necessary to create a great screen story, they should remain fluid, permitting us to move off obvious paths into realms that hold surprises for ourselves and for our readers and audiences.

Prior to developing the complete story — as a step after conceiving the initial notion — work on the character's background. Discover who and what makes up the psychodynamics of the man, woman, or child.

If we do not remain aware of the motives driving our characters, they can turn into two-dimensional, uninteresting caricatures. If our characters do not have fully realized personalities, we may discover not only that the audience loses interest, but that we lose interest in pushing the character and therefore lose the impetus behind the story.

EXERCISES

1. Prepare a one-page biography of the main character in your
   screenplay. Include:

   - Personality

   - Origins

   - Family

   - Education

   - Goals

2. Write the biography of the main character from one of your
   favorite films.

CHAPTER THREE

STORY DEVELOPMENT

Once we develop the biography of our main character or characters, the next step takes the form of a brief outline of the story. However, good stories need more than ideas. They require execution.

The difficulty arises when we have to actually write the story. The daunting task of creating new worlds and new characters lies ahead of us as if we were Hannibal (the Carthaginian general, not Lecter) on our elephants crossing the Alps. A plan exists that can make it much easier to navigate the shoals and reefs of creativity.

CLASSIC STRUCTURE

The structure that many writers use to create their screen stories is based on traditional tale-telling. This myth-legend-folk tale paradigm appears to work most of the time. First proposed by Aristotle in his *Ars Poetica*, Vladimir Propp later codified it in his work *Morphology of Folklore*. Joseph Campbell modified and amplified it in *The Hero With A Thousand Faces*. It suggests that most stories break down into three basic set pieces or acts.

In Act One protagonists are called to action, often reluctantly.

In Act Two protagonists take action, have conflicts with antagonists, take something of material or psychological value (reward, treasure, love, etc.), and then run into trouble.

In Act Three protagonists overcome adversaries and solve the conflict.

Within that structure you can find almost every story ever written, since we can ascribe wide latitude to each one of the elements. Only the writer decides what kind of action lies ahead. Only the writer determines the conflict, the nature of antagonists, the type of reward (personal, property, psychological, etc.) involved, and what kind of trouble ensues. Only the writer can solve the dilemma or dilemmas set up throughout the story.

BUILDING BLOCKS

Once we know our basic direction, the next step becomes the development of an outline called **beats**. Beats represent defining moments in the story or screenplay. For example, *Shakespeare in Love* (1998) written by Marc Norman and Tom Stoppard, begins with a beat in which the Rose Theater's financier, Fennyman, threatens the theater owner, Henslowe, who ends up promising the financier that Shakespeare has a new comedy.

That beat sets the tone for the entire motion picture. Beats can also be viewed as **megascenes** or large blocks of action linking together smaller moments in the story in order to pull the whole structure together. Those smaller bits and pieces fill out the story for us. The above scene from *Shakespeare in Love* includes the imminent torture of Henslowe; information about the state of theater in sixteenth-century London; the attitude of producers and theater owners toward actors and playwrights; and a contemporary tone established for a time that existed over 400 years ago.

BEATS FOR ACT ONE
"SHAKESPEARE IN LOVE"

1. Fennyman attacks Henslowe, who informs him that Will Shakespeare has a new comedy.
2. Will fakes it. He goes to his shrink with multiple personal complaints.
3. Whitehall Palace. A performance of "Two Gentlemen of Verona" before Queen Elizabeth. In the audience, Viola de Lesseps, enamored with Will's words. Another in the audience: the cynical, cruel Lord Wessex.
4. De Lesseps home. Viola wants poetry in her life (the first inkling of a "Romeo and Juliet" theme).
5. A depressed Will meets Marlowe, who glibly provides ideas that may help Will.
6. Viola, disguised as a boy, Thomas Kent, auditions for Will. Will pursues "Tom" to the de Lesseps house.

I don't have the slightest idea if Norman and Stoppard bothered to create beats for their clever screenplay. The above represents a breakdown as I see it.

Act One has six major beats that describe the story in very broad strokes. Little if any of the wit and humor comes through because the writers develop all of that in the treatment and refine it in the screenplay.

Some writers list beats on pages. Others use index cards. Many writers use software programs that emulate index cards. The form depends on our comfort level. No matter how we organize them, the major question we have to ask turns on whether the order of the beats makes sense in terms of the story we wish to write.

At first blush — or in the first crush of creativity — beats may appear to follow their own logic. Only later, when viewed from a distance, beats or megascenes may appear as if they need realignment.

Perhaps beat five should come after beat two. Try it out. If that doesn't work, put it back where you wrote it in the first place, remove it altogether, or use it elsewhere.

Beats, similar to school essay or thesis step outlines, provide us with a grand overview of the whole story indicating direction as well as important plot points. Megascenes become the first stop on the road to developing the story and plot.

After we have the basic story line down using the broad strokes above, the process of filling in the blank spaces begins in earnest.

Return to the notion of the three-act structure when you embark on writing the fleshed-out story or treatment. Since you already wrote the biography of your character leading up to the point where the screenplay begins, you have the first building blocks of the story. The motivations of the characters, the manner in which the character might act under a given set of circumstances, the various facets of the character often determine the story's direction.

A simplified version of the three-act structure reads:

Act One: the setup for the coming conflict
Act Two: the conflict itself
Act Three: the resolution of the conflict

This version does not provide much in the way of explanation. On the other hand, the Joseph Campbell version tends to over-intellectualize the process. So let's define structure in another way: Every good story has a problem that the protagonist must solve.

In Act One the problem presents itself. The protagonist must make a decision. Will he/she take on the task? Since this is storytelling time, of course the protagonist decides to go for it, even unwillingly. The decision to do so may come at considerable personal cost physically or psychologically, but something drives the hero into undertaking the assignment.

Act Two ratchets up the excitement by throwing a multitude of hurdles in front of the protagonist. The hero faces enemies (those enemies may not be traditional villains, but internal demons such as self-doubt, fear, or imagination). Somewhere in the middle of Act Two, the protagonist should stare into the eyes of danger. Again, it could be physical danger or psychological terror where everything seems lost until the hero breaks through the wall, carrying with him or her the long sought after real or psychic treasure. An incident that throws everything out of kilter usually occurs at the end of Act Two. It appears as if the game has ended and there's no way the protagonist can recover.

In Act Three the protagonist comes back, perhaps not immediately, but by the middle of the act the hero has crawled, fought, or clawed his/her way out of the pit and discovered the solution to the conflict or the problem that presented itself at the beginning of Act One. It could be love lost and found, a dangerous situation thwarted, reconciliation with another or with self, or any number of permutations on a theme.

THE FORK IN THE ROAD

In each scene and in each act, we should always ask the question "What if?" That prevents us from taking the easy road or the obvious path to the development of conflict and its resolution. What if the character takes the left fork in the road instead of the right? What if the character decides to trade in his or her airline ticket at the last minute? What if the character accepts a drink from a stranger? All those "what ifs" create opportunities for the story to spin off in interesting and fascinating directions and still remain consonant with the character and the rules of the world we create.

The "what ifs" become plot points within the story itself. The plot points or particular incidents fill in the spaces between the megascenes or beats. They present the writer with twists and turns, cul-de-sacs and false clues, foreshadowing events and shocks that make up the body of the treatment. They may all find themselves in the screenplay or, as in many cases, we may toss them aside because they hinder rather than help the progress of the story.

Most plot points or incidents arise out of the quandaries in which the characters find themselves. By keeping those in the forefront, we will develop solid character-driven stories. Unless the characters sit in the driver's seat, the story may unfold mechanically with little human interest to hold the audience's attention.

Too often neophyte writers come down to the third act and want to insert a new character or a piece of action that has no relationship to anything that went on before. As a result, the reader/audience can become disoriented.

Writers in those cases use what I call "writer's convenience." That's another way of saying a new element with little or no connection to anything that occurred previously has been introduced to up the ante or explain a situation. Story elements or character revelations must have justification. They should not occur just because at that moment we decide they look or sound good. Every part of a scene ought to assist in driving the story forward. Even if the moment seems strange and out of place, it must resonate with the viewer so that it makes sense within the context of the screenplay story.

FORESHADOWING AND SUBTEXT

Since characters and their stories often take on a life of their own, insights may appear from time to time. When that happens we have to dive back into the story and add, rewrite, or reconfigure so that those insights and moments unfold something new about characters or stories and feel as if they belong there.

Foreshadowing plays a critical part in accomplishing this feat. Clues to what may happen in the future often help audiences understand the actions, reactions, and motivations of our characters. That understanding may take place on a conscious or on an unconscious level. When the reader/viewer comes across a twist he/she ought to react with surprise, but surprise based on foreknowledge.

The synapses will fire up and ideas will connect when the clues you provided ahead of time become apparent. Without those clues you will astonish your reader/viewer who will then have to pause and wonder "Where the hell did that come from?"

While concentrating on the main thrust of the story becomes our primary concern, another concern is the careful development of the story's subtext. The treatment can assist us in accomplishing this with finesse.

Subtext indicates the underlying theme of the story — the unsaid, unconscious morality tale that stories require to stand the test of time. Under most circumstances subtext moves through the story with quiet determinism.

For example, a writer may wish to explore the theme of egocentric male chauvinism and its ramifications in the world of male-female relationships. Out of that motif rose *The Tao of Steve* (2000), a romantic comedy written by Duncan North and Greer Goodman & Jenniphr Goodman. On the surface, the film highlights an over-weight young man who purportedly uses Asian philosophy as his guide for seducing women. The subtext of *The Tao of Steve* examines his empty, unhappy life as he explains away his lack of commitment based on that same philosophy.

East Is East (1999), which Ayub Khan-Din adapted from his play, initially comes off as a comedy when a Pakistani father living in England tries to arrange marriages for his children. The subtext deals with the universal immigrant experience involving the fears of acculturation and assimilation and loss of identity on the part of foreignborn parents.

The irony of *East Is East* plays on the fact that the father has married a white English woman and therefore presents to his children the exact opposite of his own desires.

In both of these films the subtext, which has simmered in the background, only becomes apparent in the last part of the third act when all the angst, fears, and doubts of the characters bubble to the surface. While the stories may not end tidily, the subtexts of the tales become the forces that make the motion pictures satisfying.

SUMMING UP

By creating megascenes or beats as well as developing the intricacies of plot based on character idiosyncrasies, we can establish the story's direction and provide ourselves with the tools necessary for writing the successful screenplay. Once we lay down the foundation it becomes much easier to expand the place or *mise-en-scène,** the attitude of characters, and the subtext of the story.

The treatment also gives us a wonderful overview of the entire process. It's as if we float in a high-altitude balloon over the landscape of the story. We can identify all the landmarks below: the movement of traffic and pedestrians, the flow of rivers, and the inlets and bays. At the same time, we recognize those elements that appear out of place, the potholes in the roads that we need to repair and not ignore, so that we don't become waylaid

---

* The setting or environment in which the story or scene takes place.

on our journey into the soul of the screenplay or go off on a meaningless side trip.

Everyone wants to rush into the creative process as fast as possible. However, taking time to develop the story to its maximum before writing those first words: "FADE IN" will pay off when it comes time to writing the satisfying phrase: "FADE OUT."

EXERCISES

- Outline the beats from an existing motion picture.

- Outline the beats in your own story.

- Determine if you have constructed a solid story. What improvements can you make?

CHAPTER FOUR

ADAPTATIONS

Literary properties such as books, short stories, and plays form the basis for many films because conservatism and caution have always been the key mantras in the motion picture industry.

In a business where excellent original screenplays languish, the preponderance of adaptations may seem strange, but a logic does exist — at least for the decision-makers.

Producers and studios reason that if someone else puts up money to publish a book or produce a play then they can't be held responsible for putting money into it, even if it fails.

Search the archives of releases over the past few years and notice how many adaptations have found their way to the screen. Some recent examples are *The Cider House Rules* (1999) adapted by John Irving from his own novel; *The Perfect Storm* (2000) adapted by William D. Witcliff from the novel by Sebastian Junger; *Silence of the Lambs* (1991) from the book by Thomas Harris adapted by Ted Tally; *The End of the Affair* (1999) adapted by Neil Jordan from Graham Greene's novel; and *Traffic* (2001) adapted by Stephen Gaghan from the British miniseries *Traffik* by Simon Moore.

In addition to contemporary or near-contemporary stories, the film industry enjoys harking back to classic novels as well. For one, they tend to adapt to the motion picture format because of their emotional and visual content. For another, since older works exist in the public domain, studios do not have to pay authors for the rights.

Among recent adaptations successfully translated to the screen is Edith Wharton's *The Age of Innocence* (1993) adapted by Jay Cocks and Martin Scorcese. This was not the first time Wharton's book became the basis for a film. A silent version was released in 1924 and the first sound version came out in 1934.

The Victorian novelist Jane Austen has fallen into favor for adaptations in recent years. Douglas McGrath adapted Austen's novel *Emma* (1996) and Emma Thompson wrote the screenplay for *Sense and Sensibility* (1995).

The use of published works as the basis for screenplays, as evidenced by *The Age of Innocence* and other films, has gone on since the introduction of film. As early as 1908, Charles Dickens' *A Christmas Carol* entered the nickelodeons of the day. A few years later in 1917 his *Great Expectations* made its first foray onto the silent screen.

Not only novels, but also plays end up on the screen in a number of forms. Philip Barry's *The Philadelphia Story* (1940), adapted by David Ogden Stewart, became a major motion picture that won the screenwriter an Academy Award and James Stewart an Oscar for Best Actor. Years later, the same play became the film musical *High Society* (1956) written by John Patrick. That only proves that adaptations can venture off in different directions.

Producers even adapted the language-dependent *Hamlet* for the silent screen in 1912. While the silent version of *Hamlet* may not seem a very good choice, in recent years Shakespeare has found a place on the screen. *Henry V (1989), Richard III (1995), Hamlet (1996), Romeo and Juliet (1996), A Midsummer Night's Dream (1999)* all have a new life with vast audiences in motion picture theaters throughout the world.

CINEMATIC FAITHFULNESS

Writers developing screenplays based on another medium face the inevitable question: "How faithful must I remain to the original story?"

The pitfalls usually revolve around the reality that other people who eventually will view the film may have made up their minds about the look, sound, and feel of characters and their environment.

That dilemma confronts the makers of *Harry Potter and the Sorcerer's Stone* (2001) adapted by Steven Kloves from the best-selling, highly popular young adult novel by J. K. Rowling. Every boy and girl and many adults who have read the book and its sequels have their own version of Harry. Rowling's explicit descriptions, ranging from the young wizard's hair to his eyeglasses, have been spelled out with the smallest detail. The illustrations in the books also influence the way the characters and settings of stories appear to readers.

Everyone who has read the book and its sequels will search for errors. Depending on whether the adaptation catches the inner essence of the characters and their story, Kloves, director Chris

Columbus, and Warner Bros. will find themselves inundated by either irate missives or love letters.

The difficulty of adapting a favorite story has happened before. *Gone with the Wind* (1939), based on the novel by Margaret Mitchell and adapted by Sidney Howard, along with uncredited writers Ben Hecht, John Van Druten, Jo Swerling, and David O. Selznick, ran into the same problem. Fortunately, history demonstrated that the images satisfied audiences.

DECISIONS

After reading the original material we must decide what elements within the story seem most critical. In order to accomplish this task we have to put into place a process for cutting through the material.

A novel often deals with the interior person or story — the thoughts that form motivation or impetus for action. The screenplay ought to translate a character's internal processes into tangible action and/or dialogue in order to make them known to the audience. Once the story becomes projected on a screen, very few ways of exploring the inner workings of a character exist except through the use of voice-over narration. And that can become more of a crutch than a tool in the writer's lexicon.

The soliloquy worked for Shakespeare because he dealt with a particular theater where the actor had a vibrant, living connection with the audience. With few exceptions, the soliloquy rarely works in a motion picture.

The damning puzzle of adapting material from one medium to another involves pulling together elements that create a sense of fidelity to the original or its cinematic faithfulness in order to maintain the core of the literature within a visual medium.

Novels or short stories in the public domain have no restrictions on how far an adapter may go when making changes. Wildly free adaptations have arisen from the works of writers from Shakespeare to Jane Austen.

The caveat to that comment and its similarity to contemporary novels, plays, and short stories already mentioned, involves the audience's preconceived notions as to how characters look and the appearance of the settings in which the stories take place.

A wrong judgment, an attempt to move too far from the original, may create antagonism in the viewer. Worse, it may appear as hubris on the part of the screenwriter who makes major changes in the story.

Contemporary novels and short stories always have advocates who complain at the slightest alteration. They readily point out omissions in characters, subplots, or even choice bits of favorite dialogue. However, the task of the screenwriter is to bring printed words to life on the screen and not merely transpose the text from prose format to screenplay format.

Having said that, writers do make vast changes to classic novels and triumph. In 1995 Amy Heckerling adapted Jane Austen's Victorian novel of manners, *Emma*, into a contemporary motion picture, *Clueless*. A year later, Douglas McGrath wrote a screenplay from the same novel, but placed it in its original late 1890s setting. Both films succeeded admirably.

THE PROCESS OF ADAPTATION

To understand the procedure of adaptation, let's examine the steps that take the writer through the process.

- Read the original material without a preconceived notion of how it might appear on screen.

- Without referring to the material, outline the salient parts of the story and how characters act and react.

- Review the material and crosscheck it against your outline.

- Add or delete story points and/or characters in reference to the underlying material.

- Rewrite the outline without reference to the original.

- On completion of the outline, prepare the treatment.

- After completing the first draft treatment, return to the underlying material and determine if tone, color, character, and motivation reflect the original author's intention as you see it.

These steps provide tremendous latitude. Since the treatment will develop into visuals, you will probably make changes in order to speed up the action or coalesce several characters into one. Some novels end on a note of incredible ambiguity. The adapter may wish to give the screen story more of a sense of finality.

In all of these instances, the adapter stands as interpreter of the material not solely as someone who echoes the original. Recreating a mirror image of the written text usually ends in failure.

We deal in two different media. Each one has its own manner of presenting a story. "An adaptation is always, whatever else it may be, an interpretation." [6]

As an example, let's examine a story that has been adapted numerous times into motion pictures, stage plays, and musicals. *David Copperfield* by Charles Dickens seems to have a perennial rebirth.

In the film version produced in 1934, written by Hugh Walpole and Howard Estabrook, it's interesting to note that the credits read "Adaptation by Hugh Walpole, Screenplay by Howard Estabrook." Although information is sparse, that credit appears to indicate that Walpole wrote the adaptation or treatment upon which Estabrook based the screenplay.

For many years Dickens' fans looked at this production as one of the most faithful adaptations ever done. The critic James Agee wrote: "Though half the characters are absent, the whole spectacle of the book, Micawber always excepted, is conveyed." [7]

Chapter Twelve of the novel contains the sequence where David, who has been living with the Micawber family, is once more left on his own as the Micawbers leave London.

---

[6] Jay Gould Boyum, *Double Exposure: Fiction into Film* (New York: North American Library, 1985), 73.
[7] John Walker, Ed, *Halliwell's Film Guide 1996* (New York: HarperCollins, 1995).

Dickens wrote:

'I shall never, Master Copperfield,' said Mrs. Micawber, 'revert to the period when Mr. Micawber was in difficulties, without thinking of you. Your conduct has always been of the most delicate and obliging description. You have never been a lodger. You have been a friend.'

'My dear,' said Mr. Micawber; 'Copperfield,' for so he had been accustomed to call me, of late, 'has a heart to feel for the distresses of his fellow-creatures when they are behind a cloud, and a head to plan, and a hand to – in short, a general ability to dispose of such available property as could be made away with.'

I expressed my sense of this commendation, and said I was very sorry we were going to lose one another.

'My dear young friend,' said Mr. Micawber, 'I am older than you; a man of some experience in life, and – and of some experience, in short, in difficulties, generally speaking. At present, and until something turns up (which I am, I may say, hourly expecting), I have nothing to bestow but advice. Still my advice is so far worth taking, that – in short, that I have never taken it myself, and am the' – here Mr. Micawber, who had been beaming and smiling, all over his head and face, up to the present moment, checked himself and frowned – 'the miserable wretch you behold.'

'My dear Micawber!' urged his wife.

'I say,' returned Mr. Micawber, quite forgetting himself, and smiling again, 'the miserable wretch you behold. My advice is, never do tomorrow what you can do today. Procrastination is the thief of time. Collar him!'

'My poor papa's maxim,' Mrs. Micawber observed.

'My dear,' said Mr. Micawber, 'your papa was very well in his way, and Heaven forbid that I should disparage him. Take him for all in all, we ne'er shall – in short, make the acquaintance, probably, of anybody else possessing, at his time of life, the same legs for gaiters, and able to read the same description of print, without spectacles. But he applied that maxim to our marriage, my dear; and that was so far prematurely entered into, in consequence, that I never recovered the expense.' Mr. Micawber looked aside at Mrs. Micawber, and added: 'Not that I am sorry for it. Quite the contrary, my love.' After which, he was grave for a minute or so.

'My other piece of advice, Copperfield,' said Mr. Micawber, 'you know. Annual income twenty pounds, annual expenditure nineteen nineteen and six, result happiness. Annual income twenty pounds, annual expenditure twenty pounds ought and six, result misery. The blossom is blighted, the leaf is withered, the god of day goes down upon the dreary scene, and – and in short you are for ever floored. As I am!'

To make his example the more impressive, Mr. Micawber drank

a glass of punch with an air of great enjoyment and satisfaction, and whistled the College Hornpipe.

I did not fail to assure him that I would store these precepts in my mind, though indeed I had no need to do so, for, at the time, they affected me visibly. Next morning I met the whole family at the coach office, and saw them, with a desolate heart, take their places outside, at the back.

'Master Copperfield,' said Mrs. Micawber, 'God bless you! I never can forget all that, you know, and I never would if I could.'

'Copperfield,' said Mr. Micawber, 'farewell! Every happiness and prosperity! If, in the progress of revolving years, I could persuade myself that my blighted destiny had been a warning to you, I should feel that I had not occupied another man's place in existence altogether in vain. In case of anything turning up (of which I am rather confident), I shall be extremely happy if it should be in my power to improve your prospects.'

I think, as Mrs. Micawber sat at the back of the coach, with the children, and I stood in the road looking wistfully at them, a mist cleared from her eyes, and she saw what a little creature I really was. I think so, because she beckoned to me to climb up, with quite a new and motherly expression in her face, and put her arm round my neck, and gave me just such a kiss as she might have given to her own boy. I had barely time to get down again before the coach started, and I could hardly see the family for the handkerchiefs they waved. It was gone in a minute. The Orfling and I stood looking vacantly at each other in the middle of the road, and then shook hands and said good-bye; she going back, I suppose, to St. Luke's workhouse, as I went to begin my weary day at Murdstone and Grinby's.

The beats in the screenplay read:

- David arrives at debtors' prison. The Guard informs him that Micawber has been released and is leaving London.

- David sits with Micawber and worries about what he will do when he remembers his aunt who lives in Dover.

- The Micawbers prepare to leave London. Micawber gives David advice regarding his future. Mrs. Micawber calls to him for a last farewell and David is left alone on the streets of London.

Several pages of the novel boil down to three brief scenes, although some of the descriptions and part of the dialogue in the chapter become elements in earlier scenes.

Much of the dialogue in the novel translates directly to the screenplay. One of the best examples is in the last beat where Micawber gives David advice. In the novel, Micawber tells David:

"My other piece of advice, Copperfield," said Mr. Micawber, "you know. Annual income twenty pounds, annual expenditure nineteen nineteen and six, result happiness. Annual income twenty pounds, annual expenditure twenty pounds ought and six, result misery."

The screenplay mirrors the dialogue with a few omissions and minor changes:

```
              MICAWBER
Copperfield, at present I have noth-
ing to bestow, but advice.  Still,
that advice is far worth taking I
have never taken it myself and am the
miserable    creature    you    behold.
Young friend, I counsel you.  Annual
income twenty pounds.  Annual expen-
diture nineteen pounds. Result: hap-
piness.     Annual    income    twenty
pounds.  Annual expenditure twenty-
one   pounds.    Result:   misery.
Farewell Copperfield.   I  shall  be
happy to improve your prospects in
case anything turns up — which I am
hourly expecting.
```

CHOICES AND DECISIONS

Walpole and Estabrook make interesting choices and those choices transmit the intent of the original even though the internal monologues do not appear. Instead, the descriptions offered by the narrator (David Copperfield) often become the *mise-en-scène* of the screenplay. In its own way, the 1934 adaptation of the novel demonstrates clearly that screenplays usually do not handle interior thoughts and monologues or hidden intent very well.

Robert Nelson Jacobs* wrote the 2001 Academy Award-nominated screenplay of *Chocolat*, adapted from Joanne Harris' novel. While keeping the intention of the original, Jacobs made major changes in character and style.

Regarding style, Harris wrote the novel from two different points of view. Chapters, often alternating, tell the story from the heroine's, Vianne Rocher's, perspective and also from the perspective of the uptight local priest, Pere Reynaud.

Most of the novel involves an internal dialogue from each of these characters as they move through the story. Reynaud's narrative takes place in a hospital room as he talks to his comatose bishop. Not exactly a cinematic highlight.

Jacobs chose to tell it in a more traditional narrative style. "While this structure of competing-first-person accounts works well in the novel, I needed to find a simpler — more cinematic — way of telling the story," Jacobs explains.[8]

---

* See interview in Appendix I.
[8] Robert Nelson Jacobs, "Adapting 'Chocolat' for the Screen," *Script*, Jan.-Feb. 2001, 44.

The greatest change had to do with characters. In the screenplay, Pere Reynaud becomes a young, naive priest, Pere Henri. Jacobs created a new character called the Comte de Reynaud, mayor of the village, who has all the traits of Harris' original character.

Discussing the changes, Jacobs states, "I changed the character of Reynaud from a priest to a nobleman — the Comte de Reynaud — because I wanted to create a character who exerted power over all aspects of the townspeople's lives: political, economic, cultural, and religious." [9]

Jacobs believed that the change from priest to mayor freed him from the constraint of dealing only with the religious aspects of the novel's struggle between Vianne and Reynaud.

With all these alterations, Jacobs maintains the irony of the story along with its sense of hope set against a melancholy background. The adaptation of *Chocolat* is an excellent example of how a screenplay can become an entity in itself and still offer a sense of the original.

"A screenwriter, I believe," writes Jacobs, "must not worry too much about being 'faithful' to a book. If you follow the book too closely, you run the risk of creating the filmic equivalent of Monarch Notes: a mere study guide to the novel, an arid recapitulation with no life of its own." [10]

---

[9] Ibid., 45.
[10] Ibid., 63.

SUMMING UP

Adaptation requires the ability to take a form that explores internal issues and visualize them to the general audience. A screenwriter who believes that adaptations make life easier because the story already exists, may head for a disappointing fall when faced with the reality of recreating the story for another medium.

As much skill goes into converting the novel or short story to film as the process of writing an original screenplay. Before attempting a full-length adaptation, writers ought to try their hands at creating a film of eight to twenty minutes in length adapted from a short story.

EXERCISES

Write a brief treatment based on a short story.

- Make sure it has a beginning, a middle, and end.

- Understand what the story is *about* (every story informs).

- Develop characters that have genuine motivations for their actions.

CHAPTER FIVE

LONGFORM

The first four chapters described how writers use treatments to solve problems or sell their ideas before committing to the screenplay.

Treatments have always been a necessity in television. Usually they become part and parcel of a writer's contractual obligation since most television deals are arranged as step deals.

In a typical step deal the writer prepares a story (treatment) and gets paid for it according to the Writers Guild Minimum Basic Agreement.* At that point, the producer can "greenlight" the television script or remove the writer from the project. The same thing can happen at first draft as well.

Treatments for Movies of the Week (MOWs) on network television represent a program that covers a two-hour time span. However, the actual playing time less commercial and station breaks comes to approximately 88 minutes. For pay-per-view, the time approximates that of a feature film or approximately 120 minutes.

---

* When a writer in motion pictures and television works for a signatory to the WGA Minimum Basic Agreement (MBA), he/she must be paid at least the minimum based on a scale of payments negotiated between the Guild and the producers. That does not indicate whether a writer will be paid *over scale*. Over scale payments usually are determined when writers and their representatives negotiate the contract.

The difference in writing treatments where commercials and station breaks exist and those where there are none resides in the notion of act breaks. The former has seven acts. The latter has no act breaks for commercials; therefore the television treatment and script look the same as a feature screenplay.

With a typical network or syndicated MOW, the end of each act where the commercial or station break occurs should have a hook strong enough to bring the viewer back to the program. Although an artificial conceit designed for a medium that relies on advertising for its support, having a twist every ten or twelve minutes increases suspense and provides much needed surprises in the story. So even without artificial breaks, writers ought to create twists and surprises that drive the characters and stories forward.

The first goal in writing a treatment for an MOW is to create a viable story that intrigues an audience. However, the reality, as William Goldman clearly puts it in his book *Adventures in the Screen Trade: A Personal View of Hollywood and Screenwriting*, is that your first priority is selling it to the buyer: the producer or the production company.

Therefore the story has to contain elements such as strong characterizations, well-motivated characters; it must be a story that addresses emotions and has universal appeal that attracts the people with the money.

That's a tall order for any writer. It's much easier to have the producer hand the assignment over. In either case — pitching an original idea or receiving an assignment — creating a story that works becomes the prime consideration.

CREATING THE LONGFORM STORY

A case history of an MOW I wrote a few years ago describes the process in practical terms.

A production company requested that I prepare a treatment and script based on the true story of a priest who fought against great odds to build a shelter for the homeless.

I read all the news stories about the personality and the problems that he faced over a period of several years. Then I traveled to the location where the story took place and interviewed his friends and his associates. I researched the shelter, absorbing as much of the atmosphere as possible as well as discovering why my hero and those who worked with him entered this line of work.

After doing the groundwork, the priest and I spent time together so I could understand his personality and his almost obsessional drive to push against enormous odds to help the helpless.

The first step in developing the treatment involved blocking out the milestone events in the priest's life leading up to that point and outlining the circumstances involved in his life-altering challenge. This became the initial "beat sheet" describing the key moments that would become crucial to telling the story.

Beats will turn into a treatment and the treatment will become a television script. Since this represents a dynamic process, changes continually take place throughout the writing depending on the writer's vision.

The beats of the first act read as follows (changes have been made to the story to comply with copyright issues):

1. A few days before Christmas, priest shocked when he spots homeless people freezing under a bridge during a snow storm.

2. He preaches to the congregation about the homeless and receives sanctimonious responses.

3. He discovers more homeless crowded at the church door and permits them to enter for the night.

4. A wealthy parishioner who suffers from alcoholism turns up in a hospital. The priest visits.

5. On Christmas Eve the priest uses all of his own money to feed poor.

6. Media show up when they get word that the church has become a refuge.

7. Another wealthy parishioner condemns the priest for ruining Christmas by having homeless people sitting in the pews.

The beats provide only the basic steps in order to give me direction. The treatment fills in the spaces. More than that, the treatment also furnishes the emotional and psychological edge to the story so that it sells itself. The treatment should have all the drama, intrigue, and character development that goes into the final screenplay. If it's done well, then writing the screenplay becomes much easier.

Based on the outline, Act One of the treatment reads:

Dark, threatening clouds loom over jagged snow-covered peaks casting ominous winter shadows on the river. JACK BALDWIN drives along the river. Christmas lights adorn homes, sparkle along parkways, flash on office buildings. His headlights catch sight of people huddling against freezing weather beneath concrete spans. He peers over a retaining wall. More bodies cringe below for warmth under cardboard and rags.

(This sets the scene providing a sense of danger and misery amidst the gaiety of the season. It also provides clues that will turn up in the body of the story. At this point we don't know Jack Baldwin's identity.)

The snowstorm heightens. Jack stumbles into the entry of his home. DAVE COLSON, rough, tough, street-smart, and Jack's close friend, rails at him for not taking care of himself. Beside that — 'You're almost late for Mass.'

Jack, Father John Baldwin, stands on the altar of his church dressed in priestly vestments. He changes his sermon and talks about the plight of those he saw along the river. Something has to be done about it.

After services, one of the parishioners, a real estate developer, thanks him for reminding them of the poor who need help. It's too bad no place exists to shelter them. The Poor Box receives an extra dollop of cash.

(We discover that Jack is a priest with a heart. His parish caters to a moneyed clientele.)

Late that night, Jack lies awake restless and torn by the memory of human beings clinging sordidly to life in sharp contract to the city garbed in Christmas decorations. He walks to the church a few yards away. Near the entrance he discovers several people crouched over heat vents. He throws open the church doors and wakens the men. They're disheveled, bearded, dirty, clothed in filthy rags, their feet shod with cardboard. He tells them to get inside the sanctuary.

In the Rectory one of the other priests, FATHER O'BRIEN, sees light shining in the church. He runs over and finds forty or fifty men bedding down among the pews. Has Jack gone off his rocker? He can't leave these people in the church. What about the gold items on the altar? They'll strip the place. Jack responds that if they're that bad off let them have the gold. O'Brien calls Dave who is also the church business manager and tells him Jack's over the edge.

Dave dresses quietly. BARBARA, his wife, insists he stay home. The weather's dangerous. Besides, what Jack does is his business. Dave doesn't get paid to be his guardian angel. Maybe not, answers Dave, but if it wasn't for Jack he'd still be a falling-down drunk with no future, no job — and certainly no wife and family.

Dave enters the sanctuary and the sight of all the homeless shocks him. Jack takes Dave through the church. One man rests beneath the statue of Saint Joseph. What would the saint say if he refused "room at the inn?"

What's the purpose of the church, asks Jack? If not to shelter the poor and homeless, the lost and deprived. Dave responds that he's staying there all night to make sure nothing goes wrong. Jack orders him home, but Dave refuses and beds down among the derelicts.

(The sequence reveals Jack as an iconoclast who has a burning need to put his religious creed to work. His associates have great fidelity to him. It also provides background on why Dave needs to protect Jack.)

Next morning Dave clears out the building with the help of the homeless men and women. He inspects the church and discovers a small photo near the statue of St. Joseph. It's a fingerprint-marked, dirt-smudged picture of a middle-class family: father, mother, two children. A MAN dressed in rags with a matted, dirty beard approaches and demands to have the picture back.

(Another clue that will pay off in the third act)

Jack prepares for Morning Mass. Snow still falls and he wonders where all the homeless will go during the day. Into doorways, cafes, bars, other shelters responds Dave. Jack has a novel idea percolating.

After church he receives a panicked call from the wife of a wealthy resident of the city. The police found her husband in a drunken stupor. Jack runs to the hospital and visits MAX TILDEN, financier, a man who has the American dream wrapped up. He looks like hell. Jack warns him that the next time this happens he may have to administer Last Rites. Max replies that he hasn't been on a binge in months. How many chances does he want, asks Jack? Tilden's wife, BARBARA, begs Jack to take it easy. That's the trouble, he replies. Everyone's easy on Max, but look what he's doing to his family.

(A setup for an eventual resolution that solves two problems later in the story)

Christmas Eve.

Volunteers finish putting up decorations. One of them, ANNE CRAWFORD, a news reporter for a local TV station, corners Jack. She wants to do a story on his open church for the homeless. Jack doesn't see the news in it. He only helped about fifty people. Hundreds freeze on the city streets every night. The story might convince others to open their doors as well, suggests Anne. Jack tells her to go with it.

Word travels on the grapevine and several hundred homeless show up when the church doors open again. Dave wants to know what the hell they are going to do with all those people? Jack orders Dave to use the basement. He needs food to feed the sheltered.

Along with typical derelicts, homeless families find the church. Not knowing where their next shelter or meal is coming from, they beg Jack for a place to stay. He takes the coat off his back and gives it to a young girl.

Dave informs Jack they don't have enough money in the church coffers to feed this mob. Jack writes a personal check — his entire savings!

The man who lost his photograph sneaks inside Jack's office. Dave finds him using the telephone. He throws him out.

Midnight Mass on Christmas Eve.

Hordes of reporters and television crews gather outside the church. They want pictures of the homeless. Jack lets them in and wonders how word got out so fast. Anne hasn't been on the air.

The homeless man found in Jack's office admits calling the press. He had been a businessman who ran into trouble with alcohol and a broken marriage, but he still knows some of the press. Jack orders Dave to take him to the Rectory for a shower, shave, and a suit of clothes. If he's going to meet old friends he ought to look decent.

Anne shows up with a live crew and broadcasts from the church. After Midnight Mass the real estate developer corners Jack. He's disgusted by the presence of bums. They ruined his Christmas. It's one thing to give money and sandwiches; it's another to house them where decent people worship.

Angered, Jack reminds them they just celebrated the birth of an infant of poor parents who couldn't find room and slept in a stable. Not only the clean, the washed, the affluent have a right to a place in church. Everyone has that right."

(*Presents the first time that Jack may end up having trouble with his parishioners and, by extension, with the rest of the community.*)

11*Samaritan House*, © 1988, Michael Halperin.

It took time to discover a moving and convincing opening scene that would rivet viewers and make them wonder what came next. After a lengthy interview with the priest where we explored the genesis of his shelter, the sequence rolled out. When Father Jack Baldwin witnessed the homeless freezing under a bridge near an icy river on a cold, snowy winter night his life mission changed. That became the first of several incidents that created his obsessive drive to build a shelter for the homeless.

Many of the characters were combinations of several individuals and their stories — many of which had the same elements. Using those dramatic units maintained the integrity of the story while at the same time heightening its emotional impact.

The first act introduced the possibilities inherent in the hypocrisy of those who mouth platitudes about helping the poor as long as they do not have to see or deal with them. That became a large part of the story's subtext.

Often, we create situations or ideas that offer opportunities for further development. By using the treatment as an overview, we can spot those occasions where twists and turns push the story and heighten suspense or surprise the audience.

SUMMING UP

The treatment becomes the device for the producer and the director to have an understanding of the story's characters, setting, and direction. It's much easier to make changes at this point then when the screenplay becomes a reality and concepts become more concrete.

The example on pages 55-59 presents five major steps in Act One toward the development of the story. These steps are indigenous to narrative storytelling:

- The hook to draw in the reader/audience

- The instigating incident

- The introduction of protagonist and possible antagonist

- The foreshadowing of the story's direction

- The foreshadowing of dangers and obstacles

The remainder of the treatment rolls off these initial points. When it comes time to write the actual teleplay for the MOW, changes may take place by moving incidents around, altering them, or even eliminating some incidents and substituting other notions.

Although we believe that the story should take a specific direction or have particular elements in a certain order, it "ain't necessarily so...." Writing should always remain fluid. We ought to view it as a never-ending creative process (at least until we have to turn in the script).

Prepare yourself for new ideas that may spring up at any time and do not back away from them. Out of every ten bursts of creative energy one or two may prove worthwhile. Take advantage of the joy of creation and permit yourself the indulgence — it's less fattening than chocolate.

EXERCISES

Prepare a treatment for a Movie of the Week based on a notion from a magazine, a newspaper, or from your own experience.

- Show, do not tell the story (only describe that which you can visualize).

- Develop interesting characters who relate to one another.

CHAPTER SIX

EPISODIC TELEVISION

Contracts to write episodic television usually involve a series of steps taken prior to committing a story to teleplay.

The best way to understand the process is by looking at the schedule of minimums (payments that must be paid to writers under the Writers Guild of America [WGA] Minimum Basic Agreement, the agreement signed between the WGA and television and motion picture producers).

No matter what the length of the program — fifteen minutes all the way to two hours or more — the contract calls for a breakdown that includes story or treatment, first draft teleplay and final draft teleplay. Even when a writer signs a contract to do both story and teleplay, the same breakdown applies.

The reasons given for writing a treatment prior to moving to teleplay are 1) to get a sense of story direction, casting, and location needs. If necessary, changes can be made that would affect the outcome of the teleplay and the production; and 2) so that producers can cut off the writer if he or she does not appear appropriate for the particular story.

Unfortunately the latter can be used indiscriminately. However, in the majority of cases it doesn't come into play since the choice of writers usually is based on previous work, relationships with producers, and other factors. In addition, minimum compensation for the treatment equals approximately thirty-six percent of the total minimum compensation. Therefore, it does not make good economic sense to cut off the writer except for a compelling reason.

Principal television genres are one-hour episodic and half-hour episodic (sitcoms, dramedies). Other time lengths exist, but those have been dealt with in previous chapters.

THE ONE-HOUR EPISODIC

One-hour episodic television series fall into a number of categories: dramas such as *The West Wing, Law & Order* (and all of its permutations), *The Practice, Ally McBeal* (a hybrid dramedy); action/adventures such as *Xena* and *Walker, Texas Ranger*; or science-fiction programs such as *The X-Files* and *Buffy the Vampire Slayer*.

Some of these programs hold to a strict four-act scenario. Others use the four-act plus a teaser at the beginning and a tag at the end or a combination where a teaser is used without a tag or a tag is used without the teaser. The treatment or story must include all elements.

If the one-hour series happens to be syndicated, there may be five acts because of the increase in commercial breaks. In the case of non-commercial pay-cable television with no commercial breaks, the one-hour is written with the traditional three-act structure and no commercial breaks.

No one knows the series better than those who work on it everyday, season in and season out. The staff understands the nuances of every act and the fine points of the characters' interactions.

Prior to the mid-1980s a freelance writer with good credentials could bring a story idea to a series and, even if it was not right on the money, receive an assignment if it held the germ of a good story. Story editors and producers would work with writers to develop it.

As an executive story consultant on a major network series, I made it my task to see that freelancers wrote at least fifty percent of all stories and scripts. I believe that philosophy brought fresh ideas into the program so that episodes did not begin to all look alike.

That scenario no longer operates in the real world. Today, most series have large staffs. Each writer on staff has multiple deals — that is, they have contracts that call for them to write several episodes. Therefore if a series has four writers (who may have credits as diverse as Story Consultant, Producer, etc.) and a producer who writes, and each person is slated to write three scripts, then fifteen scripts have already been allocated for the season leaving only about seven for freelance assignment.

Competition for those assignments runs fierce and only writers who prepare will succeed. Freelancers have to walk in with stories that are as close to perfection as possible or they face rejection.

KNOW THE SERIES

Understand the program. Understand it not just as a viewer or someone who enjoys the drama or comedy. Any writer planning on making a pitch to a show must have a deep comprehension about the inner workings of the characters and how the creators put stories together. Therefore a systematic and organized approach should be taken when approaching any project.

You should have an intimate awareness of the series' attitude and what kind of audience the producers want to reach. Whether the program runs on a network, on cable, or in syndication will determine not only act structure but also latitude in terms of language and themes.

The steps to take before making that all-important phone call to get an appointment — or if you have an agent and want your agent to set up the pitch — are:

- Obtain a copy of the series **bible**. This document contains the premise of the series, backstories of the characters, and often delineates relationships between characters. The bible may describe the arc of the series as well as the subtext. If the series has been on the air, the bible may include synopses of previous episodes. Numerous sites on the Internet post episodes as well as valuable information for writers.

- Tape episodes and watch them over and over again so that you understand the pattern of each act. Note that on most series an archetype for the way in which acts develop will emerge providing a basic formula for the program. (This is not an absolute.)

- If possible, obtain copies of several teleplays and study them thoroughly.*

- Determine what each act accomplishes. For example, does the first act introduce the heavy? Does the second act develop

---

*The Writers Guild of America library (7000 W. Third St., Los Angeles, California 90048) houses screenplays and teleplays that may be read on the premises. Other sources for teleplays are specialized services that provide screenplays and teleplays for a fee. A few Web sites have screenplays and teleplays on their pages. Rarely will a series provide freelance writers with script copies, but it does no harm to contact the show and request them.

a particular relationship between characters? How does the third act heighten the excitement that draws the audience into the fourth act?

- Examine how heroes propel the story forward in each of the acts. Freelancers often fall prey to the temptation of introducing a new character who may take control of the story. New characters almost always play second fiddle to the main characters or heroes of the story. That's why they are the heroes and the stars of the show and get paid the big bucks!

- Understand how each act typically ends. On a high note? A low note? Suspense? Comedy?

- Analyze character backgrounds in order to determine what makes each character unique. Use the series' bible. It usually provides biographies of the main characters (see Chapter Two, p.16).

- Assess the roles of characters within the series as a whole and how they play out within a variety of episodes. (The necessity to tape several episodes becomes apparent.)

- Determine the function of each of the regular characters in the series. Remember: They exist for a reason. The main character or characters drive the story forward. Other characters may act as foils for the main character or for purposes of comic relief, or to explain some of the inner workings of the particular environment in which the series takes place (law office, hospital, police precinct, etc.).

- Have an understanding of the pattern and the pace of the series. Determine the average number of scenes in each act. Estimate the average page length of each act. That information will tell you the average length of the overall script. An action-oriented script usually is shorter than a dialogue-heavy script.

- Identify the attitude of the series. Many series are easy to categorize as realistic, gritty, comedic, dramatic, or a combination of two or more of those categories.

- Know the audience for which the series is intended. Demographics can be important in terms of the types of stories told. In addition, the time slot in which the series airs also informs you of the kind of language you can use and the themes you can explore in episodes.[*]

- Pay attention as to whether the series plays on a network (CBS, NBC, ABC), a Fox Network type outlet, syndication, cable, or pay-cable. Each one has its own peculiarities in regard to censorship, language used, themes covered, etc.

- Understand the **megatheme** of the series. That represents the overarching motif of the show. As an example, in the NBC series *Law & Order* the theme of the series is expressed in the opening narrative: "In the Criminal Justice System the people are represented by two separate, yet equally important groups: the police who investigate crime and the District Attorneys who prosecute the offenders. These are their stories."

---

[*] In general, an 8 p.m. series deals with lighter themes and less gritty language than a 10 p.m. show although that isn't always the case. View the series and note if it follows that rule.

- Know the subtext of the series. While the megatheme presents the overt motif of the series, the subtext delves into the underlying agenda in terms of its personal stories. The subtext usually has more to do with the success or failure of a series than any other element.

PREPARING THE PITCH

After following this procedure, the next step toward developing a story for an existing series is the **notion** or the **pitch.** The pitch embodies the basic elements of a story in a very concise form.

The pitch itself is a one-paragraph version of your story. It should have a beginning, middle, and end that can be told within two or three minutes. Have it memorized or on an index card so that you do not forget any salient points. However, if you use index cards, do not read from them. Only use them as a reminder. Lead off your pitch with a *TV Guide*-type caption: an intriguing one-sentence line that will pique the interest of producers, story editors, and story consultants.

Be prepared to discuss your story. The staff will no doubt make many suggestions. Tape-recording the story conference permits you to engage in the creative free flow of ideas without resorting to pen and paper or laptop. Make sure you receive permission for taping the conference from those in attendance. No one likes to be caught saying something they may regret later. On the other hand, if someone in a position to give you an assignment tells you to write the story and bring it in, that's tantamount to receiving the go-ahead.

According to the Writers Guild Minimum Basic Agreement, "If in the first interview the writer gives a story, then a second meeting at the request of the Company concerning that story shall constitute a story commitment at minimum compensation…"

In addition, "If at the request of the Company the writer gives a story, either by telephone or in person or otherwise, then a meeting on that story at the request of the Company is a commitment." [12]

Sometimes a pitch comes about as the result of a new insight the writer may have into the characters. The very first episode I wrote for *Falcon Crest* came in its first season. I wrote it before the series ever aired. The creator and producer of the show, Earl Hamner, provided me with the first few scripts, the bible of the show, and videotapes of the first episodes.

It occurred to me that no one addressed the fact that a woman, Angela Gioberti Channing (played by Jane Wyman), headed the winery. She inherited it from her father even though she had an older brother. It seemed peculiar to me that in an Italian family of that period, the estate would go to a female.

Perhaps a story that wove the current story line with Angela's past could work. It would explain her tough, rigid attitudes because she has to prove more worthy than any son. Earl agreed and asked me to write the story encompassing the threads already developed.

WRITING THE ONE-HOUR EPISODIC TREATMENT

The treatment for the *Falcon Crest* episode "House of Cards" went

---

[12] Writers Guild of America Basic Agreement, Article 20.B (c) (d)

through several revisions. What follows are sections of the treatment that fulfill one of the goals of the episode: to explain Angela, but without making the story into a psychological exposé or essay.

Part of the story in the first season dealt with the death of Jason Gioberti, brother of Angela Gioberti Channing, owner of Falcon Crest. He died in an accident, but Angela believes that her daughter, Emma, had something to do with it. Since Jason's death Emma went off the deep end — sometimes into a psychotic state. Angela tried to protect her. Others in the family bring a psychiatrist to the estate in order to help Emma. Angela discovers the subterfuge.

In Scene 2 of Act 3, Angela warns her older daughter, Julia, that if the truth comes out they could lose everything. "Angie worked too damned hard — her brain, muscle and sweat have gone into the land and no upstart's going to take it away from her." [13]

That comment is the first inkling into Angela's tough, no-nonsense attitude to everyone and everything around her.

The next escalation in discovering Angela's subtext comes in Scene 1, Act 4. Suspecting that Falcon Crest may slip away, she confronts Julia once more when her daughter insists that "Falcon Crest isn't a home. It's a place, a sterile state of mind made emptier by Angie's obessiveness… Angie grasps her daughter's arm and thrusts her into a chair. Angie shakes with emotion for the first time in a long while. 'You don't know me. You don't know me at all,' she says passionately."

That extends into Scene 3, Act 4 when Angela explains how she worked with her grandfather and father to make Falcon Crest into

---

[13] Michael Halperin, *Falcon Crest*, "House of Cards," Dec. 15, 1981, © Warner Bros. Television, 15.

one of the great estates: "Angie worked the fields and dug irrigation ditches and drove the tractors. It hardened her. It made her part of the land. The earth is in her blood..." [14]

The story went through several permutations with scenes added, scenes dropped, and characters changed. This occurs in almost every writing project. The rewrite process, whether at the treatment stage or the script stage, plays one of the most critical parts in the development of a story. For television, it becomes important because of budgetary considerations, locations, or time. Therefore some components of an act or scene may need adjustments.

While the *Falcon Crest* scenes have quite a bit of detail, some producers prefer shorter and tighter descriptions. Others want expansive treatments that leave little doubt as to the visual and dialogue components of the finished teleplay.

The basic treatment format for hour or half-hour episodic shows is the same. However, if it's a comedy, it better read funny — on paper and in the teleplay.

---

[14] Ibid, 22.

SUMMING UP

Before beginning the process of writing for any television series, follow the edict: Know the series.

Understand the attitude, style, and audience for which the show is intended. Become familiar with the differences between network, syndication, basic cable, and premium cable needs.

Prepare yourself by taping episodes and making breakdowns of all the essential ingredients that go into making the series viable and successful.

Recognize the relationships between the various characters — especially the main characters — and how they drive the series.

EXERCISES

1. Develop a treatment for your favorite one-hour episodic television drama.

2. Develop a treatment for your favorite half-hour sitcom.

For each of the above you should:

- Understand the series.

- Prepare a scene-by-scene breakdown of each act.

- Outline the relationships between characters.

- Prepare a 2-3 minute pitch of your story.

CHAPTER SEVEN

DAYTIME SERIALS — THE SOAPS

Daytime serials, colloquially called "soap operas," are a unique genre.

They originated in the earliest days of commercial radio. Many of the radio soaps lasted until 1960. A few of them became television series as early as 1952 (*The Guiding Light*), using the same format and story lines that audiences had listened to for a generation or more.

Some of the most popular daytime serials on radio had titles such as *Backstage Wife* ("The story of Mary Noble and what it means to be the wife of a famous Broadway star, dream sweetheart of a million other women."); *Our Gal Sunday* ("The story of an orphan girl named Sunday, from the little mining town of Silver Creek, Colorado, who in young womanhood married England's richest, most handsome lord..."); *Stella Dallas* ("A continuation on the air of the true-to-life story of mother love and sacrifice..."); and *The Brighter Day* ("Our years are as the falling leaves... we live, we love, we dream... and then we go...").

The opening narration of *The Brighter Day* sounds very familiar. The current television soap *Days of Our Lives* opens with "Like sands through the hourglass so are the days of our lives."

One definition of the soap opera is a "serialized dramatic television broadcast daily… usually during the afternoon." [15]

While someone once commented that daytime serials seem to never begin and never end, they all have a beginning — a genesis — important to the structure of the story and its characters.

Almost every one of these daily daytime programs moves at a rather leisurely pace in order to assist viewers, the majority of whom are women, to keep track of various story lines. However, over the past fifteen or twenty years soaps have become popular among college students. Since they can't always watch every episode, the slow pace suits their lifestyle as well.

Because of the pressure to deliver five episodes a week, the soap infrastructure dictates the manner in which teleplays develop.

Soaps have staff writers called either Outline Writers or Assistant Head Writers, Dialogue Writers, Assistant Writers; sometimes they employ freelance writers. Leading the creative effort are Head Writers.

Head Writers develop a document called a **long-term projection** that can be compared to extensive treatments. It outlines the direction of the series over a protracted period of time. Outline Writers use the projection and prepare outlines or treatments for each episode. After approval of the outlines, Dialogue Writers prepare teleplays based on the outlines.

---

[15] M. G. Cantor and S. Pingree, *The Soap Opera* (Beverly Hills, CA: Sage Pub., 1983.)

The necessity for doing that becomes apparent when you look at the multitude of characters with multiple problems and interlocking stories playing out over a prolonged period of time.

LONG-TERM PROJECTIONS

Since soaps go on for years it's important to have a firm grasp on the intent of the show. Therefore a long-term projection presents both the overt agenda as well as the subtext for six months or longer depending on the particular series.

Writers who prepare projections — usually Head Writers, but sometimes experienced freelancers — have to have a deep familiarity with the program, especially the relationships that exist between various characters. Soaps for the most part depend on relationship stories for their impact. Writers must know what stories have been developed in the past and what's happening at the moment.

They should know the philosophy behind the soap — usually expressed by the opening narration, although that may provide only a small window into the interior working of the series.

The projection ought to outline not only the intertwined stories but also a sense of where the story and characters will go after this period of time. In other words, the projection provides opportunities for future stories.

CREATING THE PROJECTION

The same process that functions for developing stories for one-hour episodics or sitcoms operates for creating long-term projections.

If the Head Writer does not write the projection, then individuals who have experience with soaps or similar dramas including episodic television, film, novels, or plays are brought in to provide fresh perspectives.

In all of these instances writers must have an intimate understanding of the show including its minutiae and its trivia because stories in soaps often spin off of such things.

Writers who comprehend characters and plotting will do well with projections. Writers who take a long view of the story development will also do well.

In a way, soaps and their projections foreshadowed the kind of nonlinear writing that we can compare to computer-generated game play. The big difference occurs in outcomes. While a computer-based game provides a variety of options at each story nexus, in soaps decisions have been made on the direction the story will take. However, as in computer games, when stories intersect in daytime serials, writers of projections can make any number of choices.

While individual stories involving specific relationships have classic beginnings, middles, and ends, each one must tie in to other stories within the series. Common elements should be woven throughout the projection. Only in that way will the series retain its cohesive nature.

THE WRITING PROCESS

Writers have very little freedom to innovate with soaps. Head Writers prepare story lines and it's up to the Outline Writers to follow their lead without too many deviations. Dialogue Writers must stick to the Outline assiduously. Viewers of soaps have long memories and want their characters to act appropriately. The need for consistency of character and the ways they act, react, and interrelate has almost everything to do with the success of daytime serials.

Story lines extend over long periods of time with digressions, bypaths, and dead ends that have shorter time spans.

In most cases Story Editors will edit and revise almost every episode that goes on the air. While many primetime television and feature writers resent having others rewrite them, soap writers accept rewrites as a fact of life.

Head Writers place their stamp on the show. With so many episodes and so many writers, they and the Story Editors provide consistency of style as well as a vision of the program's progress.

SUMMING UP

Writing for daytime serials entails a different mindset from almost every other type of writing for television.

If you happen to be fortunate and graduate to the realm of Head Writer you have a daunting task. The job placed before you consists of having a profound understanding of the past, present, and future direction of the show. That knowledge must find its way into the development of long-term projections that guide the series through five episodes a week for up to six months or a year at a time.

Everyone writing for daytime serials utilizes the long-term projection as well as story lines for each episode created by Outline Writers to prepare daily teleplays that have intrigued generation upon generation of viewers.

Writing staffs tend to be large because of the pressure to deliver five scripts a week, fifty-two weeks a year. At the time of this writing, *Days of Our Lives* has a Head Writer, seven Associate Head Writers, and four Dialogue Writers. In addition, the soap employs a number of Assistant Writers who also prepare scripts. On occasion some serials also use freelance writers.

EXERCISES

Describe your favorite soap opera with a one-page synopsis. Include:

- The environment

- The main characters

- The principal dilemmas

CHAPTER EIGHT

STRUCTURE

Once you receive the assignment to write an episode of a television series — or even if fortune smiles upon you and you become a staff writer — the time comes when you have to sit down and write the treatment or the story. How well that turns out determines whether or not you end up writing the teleplay.

Chapter Six covered the basic elements of a treatment for a teleplay. While those factors play the same for almost all screenplays and teleplays, it's important to understand what they mean and how they become indispensable to the eventual screenplay. As the architect Mies van der Rohe stated, "God is in the details."

ONE-HOUR EPISODIC

The treatment covers four acts often with a **teaser** at the beginning and a **tag** at the end. If the series is syndicated it may have five acts due to an additional commercial break.

A teaser is a brief scene that opens the episode. It serves as a device for enticing the audience into the show so they will continue to view the episode after credits roll.

For example, on the NBC series *The West Wing*, the teaser serves two functions. It reprises many of the key moments of the entire season and then brings the audience up-to-date on the current crisis of the series. Opening credits roll, the program goes to commercial and then the first act begins, usually picking up the thread of the story shown in the teaser.

The teaser also plays the role of providing a moment of exposition so those viewers who missed a previous episode will have a notion of what preceded this particular segment.

Not all teasers work the same way. It all depends on the series and its goals. In some action-adventure series, the teaser leaps out at the viewer with a strong action piece designed to titillate and excite.

On the NBC series *Law & Order* the teaser presents the instigating or inciting incident for the drama that follows — the discovery of a murder victim or a circumstance that brings the first half of the story into play leading to the eventual trial.

The acts of a typical one-hour drama or dramedy develop along these general lines:

- Act One
  Setup for the action to follow. Establishing the inciting incident so that the hero(es) can take action and follow through.

- Act Two
  Conflict develops permitting the hero(es) to enter the field of conflict and begin the battle. The battle might be an investigation, a crisis situation, a personal dilemma, etc.

- Act Three

  The conflict rises and becomes personal. The hero(es) pushes the story forward and discovers new information that will help him/her/them solve the problem presented in Act One and developed in Act Two.

- Act Four

  The hero(es) resolves the conflict after overcoming a variety of obstacles thrown in his/her/their way by antagonists.

A typical network and syndicated teleplay may run between 52 and 62+ pages (depending on whether or not it leans toward action or dialogue). The fifth act of a syndicated series is part of the fourth act with a break for an additional commercial. Each act tends to be shorter, but the page length of the teleplay remains the same.

If the series uses a tag, that brief scene may tie up some kind of personal problem. Often the tag consists of a joke to lighten the mood of an episode. On other series it may provide a moment of reflection by the main characters on what occurred during the show and present viewers with a prosocial commentary.

Quite often *The West Wing* portrays some of the characters outside of their usual White House venue commenting with due humility on their role in the democratic process.

HALF-HOUR EPISODIC (SITCOM)

The same basic formula exists for the creation of a half-hour or sitcom script. The half-hour may break down into either two or three acts. Since sitcoms spin off of jokes or comedic situations, that setup occurs in the first act, preferably within the first minute or two.

The sitcom *Frasier* has its own distinctive format, but one that derives from almost every other half-hour show since the earliest days of television and, as a matter of historic interest, radio.

What makes *Frasier* unique is the use of titles to separate scenes in the acts. The titles are additional jokes written with either an ironic twist or as a play on words.

- Act One
  Opens under titles and presents the inciting incident that sets up the rest of the story and the jokes to follow. The scene usually begins in the same place for each episode (although it may change depending on the situation). The situation develops and builds to a crisis ending in a major joke or comic event that propels the story into

- Act Two
  The crisis usually ends in a misunderstanding with the hero, Frasier in this case, receiving his comeuppance due to his superior attitude, ending in a life lesson learned about the need for humility. It can end either on a high note of humor or with a sense of pathos.

Staff writers or writer-producers write most sitcoms. In many cases, the creative staff kick around ideas, jokes, and comic situations until one notion comes out of the session that looks as if it might make a good show.

Often, they build the structure of the episode on cards or on a board. Input for situations and comic bits comes from everyone who writes, produces, or directs for the show. One of the writers receives the assignment and develops the story or treatment.

While sitcoms take place in very specific locales or with specific professions, the objective is to play humor that appeals to a broad audience.

To quote a Paramount Television publicity release: "*FRASIER is a half-hour comedy series set in Seattle, WA, which chronicles the lives of an eloquently pompous radio show host Dr. Frasier Crane, his brazen radio producer Roz, his competitive, high-brow brother Niles, their crotchety father Martin and his quirky live-in nurse Daphne.*"

Frasier is not a show about a radio psychiatrist, but uses the notion to portray an often supercilious know-it-all who has to deal with life on terms he may not like or appreciate.

The same thing holds true for shows such as *Seinfeld*. Ostensibly about the life of a comedian, it portrayed the empty lives of single urban men and women who kept trying to fill the void in their lives with meaningless trivia. In the attempt they always tripped themselves up, providing hooks for comedy.

A number of years ago a young would-be comedy writer approached me with the idea that he could write a better sitcom than those on the air because he had worked in places they portrayed.

I quickly dissuaded him of the notion by making him realize that the settings were merely background for the characters, their relationships, and their quirks, likes, and dislikes which provided the ammunition for jokes.

After all, sitcoms are all about jokes. That's why they're called situation-*comedies*.

A rule of thumb for almost all half-hour comedies is at least one joke per page. A joke can play as a wisecrack or a humorous situation. However, the joke has to relate to the story and usually plays off the inciting incident that opens the particular episode.

With sitcoms as well as hour-long episodics, it's critical to know thoroughly the quirks, fallibilities, talents, likes, and dislikes of the characters. Being a fan of a show is not enough. The writer who wishes to create a story for a series must understand the dynamics of all the relationships in the program and what motivates them.

SUMMING UP

Every hour and half-hour episodic television series has its own formula. However, almost all programs have the same structure.

The one-hour episodic usually breaks down into four acts (five if in syndication) and may have a teaser at the beginning or a tag at the end.

Half-hour episodics usually have two acts (although some may have three) with a possible teaser and tag.

The only way to determine how the show works is to study it assiduously so that you understand the fine points of each act, the characters, their relationships, their foibles, and their strengths.

Any story that you wish to create for a series has to fit within the confines of the locales and with the characters' personalities. A writer wishing to receive an assignment plays a dangerous game when he or she attempts to rewrite either the megatheme or the subtext of the series.

Basically, every story in a series is a theme on a variation. How creative you are depends on how you play that theme in a way that makes producers, story consultants, and story editors sit up and take notice.

EXERCISES

View a network, syndicated, and cable one-hour episodic television series and half-hour sitcom.

For each of them describe the variations in structure for:

- A network series

- Syndicated series

- Cable series

CHAPTER NINE

A FINAL WORD

The first words in this book told of the dismay that many writers face before they sit down to create stories that translate into exciting visual images. The final word brings together the elements necessary for the development of viable screenplays and teleplays for motion pictures and television.

Treatments or stories help us resolve enigmas that result from the first flush of the creative thrust when we push through a story. That first draft, while filled with excitement, fury, ardor, passion, and emotion, often has within it traps that can throw us into a pit with very slick walls.

By using the treatment as another device for solving the very riddles we create for ourselves, we can scale those walls and produce screenplays that have their own sense of logic.

The very nature of the stories upon which we base screenplays demands that they contain not only the basic story but also the intricacies of plot and subtext — that hidden agenda that gives scripts texture and substance.

A well-written treatment, whether it's ten or fifty pages, presents us with conflict and the resolution of that conflict as well as the interior workings of our characters, their relationships, and their motivations. Without those carefully delineated factors, stories may end up with weak characterizations, implausible plots, and holes through which a truck could drive with an SUV on either side.

Just as in any good structure, the architect (in this case the writer) needs a sound blueprint upon which to develop the final product. If well-defined and well-written, the treatment becomes the guide through the strange, amorphous world of creativity.

STRUCTURE AND METHOD

A multitude of books and a proliferation of writing seminars exist that offer formulas for success. However, the reality is that no formula exists. If it did, everyone who followed one of the proffered formulae would automatically succeed in this very difficult art/business.

The word "art" deliberately takes first place because writing is first and foremost an art form. Writers who believe in what they create and write from conviction will succeed. Those doomed to failure for the most part are writers who decide they will write whatever it takes to sell — that is, they will scramble and chase after the elusive creature called the "commercial screenplay."

Often those individuals view the current state of cinema and decide to jump on the bandwagon of fashionable trends. By the time their screenplays become a reality, the bandwagon has moved out of town and a new circus has entered Main Street. Thus what once seemed fashionable turns into an obsolete fad.

Basic structure remains paramount in the development of the story. Until writers master the three-act structure, they should not attempt to break the structure. In other words, know the rules before you disassemble them.

The three acts of any good story represent the simplest of concepts. But never construe simplicity with ease of accomplishment. From Greek tragedy to Shakespearean drama to Arthur Miller, the structure has proven effective and the plays and their characters highly complex.

Structure reveals the following:

- ACT ONE presents the setup for the upcoming conflict, including the preliminary introduction of motivation and subtle foreshadowing.

- ACT TWO provides the opportunity for developing the conflict and exploring in depth the characters and their interrelationships.

- ACT THREE offers the opening for resolving the immediate conflict as well as some notion of what may happen to the characters in the future, after "The End" appears on screen.

Developing the basic story and characters involves the creation of beats in an outline form. Beats form the largest blocks or megascenes that eventually become linked together to create the whole structure. Beats provide an overview of the entire notion and become the first elements necessary to create both story and plot.

The treatment becomes the form that brings all the elements together as a cohesive unit. Along with the main story and basic plot points arising out of the dilemma, a subtext should exist that subtly expresses the underlying theme of the story.

ADAPTATIONS

Anyone considering adapting existing material for the screen or television must decide what are the most critical elements of the story. Since many novels enter into a character's internal thoughts, writers must develop those thoughts in a tangible manner so that the audience gains a perception of the internal processes.

The key to adaptation involves creating visual elements that maintain a sense of fidelity to the original. Therefore the adapter can be seen as an interpreter who recreates, but does not mirror the original, since print and film are different media requiring different approaches.

LONGFORM

Television more than any other visual medium usually requires the writer to prepare a treatment. Just as in a theatrical film, it's necessary to create a story that intrigues the audience. After all, in the case of television, the audience has not paid a ticket price to sit in a darkened room with a few hundred others. That act alone creates in many people the need to stick with it no matter the circumstances.

Writers have to create and design each act of a Movie of the Week or a miniseries to end with a hook that brings the audience back to the story. The treatment becomes the blueprint pointing out where to place those plot points and where to heighten suspense, drama, comedy, and strengthen characterizations.

Those hooks often represent the plot points and elements that will attract producers and creative talent to the story.

An idea only exists when a writer commits it to paper. Only then does idea become story. One of the ways to create a blueprint is to block out the milestone events of the story. This becomes the "beat sheet" which describes the megascenes. The beat sheet then translates into a treatment that contains characterizations, relationships, motivations, and the through line that finds its way into the eventual screenplay or teleplay.

It's important to note that neither the beats nor the treatment exist as unchanging entities. These fluid documents only provide signposts on the road to developing the finished product. However, it does give us an opportunity to carve out the various bypasses, cul-de-sacs, and off ramps that can lead to surprises in the script.

Not every detail goes into a treatment, many treatments for a feature or longform television are eight or ten pages long. We have to leave room for the characters and the story to lead us into unexpected places (always based on the characters, their motivations, and their reasons for existing).

EPISODIC TELEVISION

This is one area where treatments have become the norm. Half-hour and one-hour television writers are expected to write treatments prior to developing the teleplay.

The main reason for the television treatment is to make sure that the story works within the confines of the series.

Before freelance writers begin developing the story, they should know the series as fully as possible. By taking a highly organized approach and using all the tools available, it's possible to gain an in-depth understanding of a particular show and begin crafting stories for it.

Writers must prepare themselves with a solid story that has a beginning, middle, and end — with each of those elements deliberately molded to the series involved.

Once the story is developed, a pitch is made that tells that story in two or three minutes. If writers do their homework, assignments may come about. Writers who deliver what producers want in creative and exciting ways can also end up on staff. Once on the inside, they discover the fine points of the series and how to fine-tune scripts so that they fit within the overall scheme of the program.

The major difference in episodic television treatments has to do with length: The series is a one-hour episodic or a half-hour sitcom.

Usually one writer develops the one-hour episodic teleplay. That means he or she creates the pitch and writes the treatment on which the script is based.

In the half-hour sitcom, development may involve the writing staff who spin the story and create jokes that work within the series' context. Then an individual writer bundles the ideas and builds the treatment.

SUMMING UP

While some writers view treatments as a necessary evil, the reality is that they can be one of the most effective tools in the creative toolbox.

They provide us with the map across the creative landscape and can indicate and highlight problems before we hit the gridlock of the imagination.

Treatments are the first major step toward the creation of screenplays or teleplays. They should never be viewed as permanent documents but as dynamic visions that change with stories, characters, and their motivations. Because these are fluid, they present the basics of the story including plot and subtext, conflict and resolution as well as the overarching theme or moral of the story in a clear, concise manner.

The treatment becomes the searchlight cutting through the darkness and highlighting moments of drama and comedy necessary to illuminate the imagination.

EXERCISES

1. Write the beats for your own story.

2. Write the treatment for your story.

Once you have completed this last exercise you're ready to sell your story — or write your million-dollar screenplay.

Good luck!

APPENDIX

I. Interviews
      Robert Nelson Jacobs, Screenwriter
      Lynn Roth, LongForms
      Jon Sherman, Sitcoms
      Al Rabin, Daytime Serials

II. Sample Treatment

III. Referenced Films and Their Writers

IV. Referenced Television Programs and Their Writers and Creators

V. Copyright and Registration

VI. "What Every Writer Needs to Know"

VII. Finding an Agent

VIII. Finding a Producer

APPENDIX I

INTERVIEWS

An Interview with Robert Nelson Jacobs, Screenwriter

Robert Nelson Jacobs wrote the screenplay of the critically acclaimed motion picture *Chocolat*, for which he received an Academy Award nomination for best screenplay adapted from another medium in 2000.

There are two distinct functions for treatments. One is the sales function and the other is the diagnostic one.

In the case of Chocolat *it was both. I was an unknown quantity to Miramax so I not only had to write the treatment to satisfy my own story requirements, I had to convince them to let me write the screenplay.*

That's different than writing something to see if the story works. However, I believe it became a very useful exercise. It made me think more about the characters than if I had done an outline for myself. Every time I sit down and force myself to write for someone else to read, I make discoveries, discoveries I wouldn't have made if I had done my own outline and started writing.

Treatments allow me to see the strengths and weaknesses in my story and work through some issues. To me structure is always the hardest part. It's the torture of the work. My impulse has always been to start writing as soon as possible. I know I'm better off if I hold myself back. The longer I wait until I start the actual writing and the more time I spend with the torture of the structure, the better off I am.

Using the treatment as a diagnostic tool, I reveal the obstacles and pitfalls to others and myself so we can discuss how to overcome them. It's a useful exercise — if I trust the opinions of the people with whom I'm working. If I do it with people I don't trust, it can become excruciating because they start pulling me in directions I don't want to go before I have a chance to show them what the movie is about.

I approach adaptations as if they are originals. To me it's the same process. I'm either working from my own unformed notion that needs shaping or working from someone else's notion that works as a book, but may not work as a movie. In that sense it's an unformed notion as well.

For example, with Chocolat *I understood that the novel needed to be changed fundamentally. My number one challenge was to open it up. I also added, subtracted, and changed characters. I tried to create a sense of an interesting ensemble — characters with whom I wanted to spend a year of my life.*

The process starts with free association. I write down ideas that don't necessarily connect with each other, notions about characters. I write things about the story that I don't know how to solve. I write down all the reasons why the project doesn't work and will never work. Once I get into the deepest level of my fears and complaints about it, then I can work through it. In other words, I start out by saying what I don't like about it. Then I'll figure out what I wish it were and find my way to what it will be. You have to live in that place for a while.

I let the ideas rattle around. It's the "what if" stage. What if this character was related to that character in a particular way? I find it extremely difficult because at that early stage I'm so unaware. But I give myself knowledge through research. There's great comfort in doing that. I have something to hold on to. My research on the history of chocolate led me to the idea of the Mayan theme in Chocolat. *That created the whole visual cinematic backstory for the main character.*

I don't like to commit to my characters right away. It's better to have lots of possibilities about who the characters might be. Since characters and plot are intertwined, I have to understand the possibilities in my characters in order to generate the plot. I also have to have ideas about plot in order to understand who my characters need to be. The more I work out the plot, the more it tells me about my characters.

Some writers hate rewriting. I love it because the story always gets better. You're no longer in that blind, stumbling place. I have a better idea of what my story's about and what it needs to be. The decisions I make are better informed. There's a real feeling of power when I'm working on the second or third draft and I understand what I'm trying to achieve.

I know that the treatment is ready when I can read it through from beginning to end and it coheres. It makes a kind of narrative sense to me. I don't stop and think, "How is that possible?" or "Why is this character doing that?" or "What does this mean?" Can I get through it without floundering over those larger questions such as motivation and fundamental meaning of the story? But it's always a test.

I once attended a fiction workshop given by John Updike in which he said that when you're looking for the end of a story, it's as though you're in a dark room looking for the door to get out. You don't know whether it's two inches in front of you or ten miles away. You just have to have faith and you keep going and looking for that door. I asked him how you know when you've found the door. He said, "Because it opens."

When I start the screenplay, I have to leave myself open to discovery. I hope that those discoveries won't throw off my structure. Sometimes an idea hits me like a bolt of lightning and it's much better than what I had. If that happens I accept it as a gift. I go back and rework the structure to accommodate the new idea.

An Interview with Lynn Roth on Longforms

Lynn Roth has written, produced and directed television series, Movies of the Week, and features. Among her credits are Executive Producer for Showtime's *The Paper Chase*; *The Portrait*, a TNT film; the CBS MOW *Patron Saint of Liars*; and ABC's MOW, *A Bunny's Tale*. In 2001 she wrote the miniseries *The Bridesmaids* for CBS.

It's a different talent to write a treatment than to write a screenplay. Treatment writing is like novel writing or journalism and a screenplay is a very different thing. Some people have the ability to write a treatment and not a screenplay. It's hard because they're two distinct types of writing. I don't feel comfortable with it. I'm much more comfortable with dialogue. But if you have too much dialogue in a treatment you can't get enough of the plot-point structure.

The treatment represents the bone-crunching part because you have to sit down with new material and put it into a structure that will show someone that there's enough to fill the allotted time — two hours for a movie, or in the case of the CBS miniseries I just finished, The Bridesmaids, *I had to be able to show them there was enough story, plot development, and character development to hold four hours of television.*

Sometimes it's hard to stick to a treatment because then it seems as if it's a formula and I feel like a secretary typing everything I figured out six months ago. I like to keep myself open for surprises. And as I spend more and more time with the characters and write their dialogue and go through their thought processes, then I see that what I put in the treatment may not have been right. I say to myself "that person would never do that... What did I think? That doesn't sound like my character." It's as if I did something because it was convenient for the treatment.

For me, the treatment represents a series of road signs. If I'm doing a scene and I know I'm headed for another scene, then I have to prepare ahead of time to get there. It tells me the exit's a half-mile down the road and I have to get in the right lane to get off. I know that if I'm in the middle of Scene 16 that I have to get to Scene 17 in a graceful and believable way.

In television, treatments become important because the structure has more rigidity and tends toward the formulaic, whereas in features it doesn't seem to have as much formality.

A treatment might have a fabulous beginning and a fabulous ending and then the middle pops up and you have to keep people from making phone calls. It definitely reveals where the problems and holes are in the story.

It's different if it's being used as a blueprint for yourself or as a selling tool. If you're doing a treatment to sell the story you have to spark it up. Even when someone has a screenplay, the producers will ask for pages. And they better be good.

The treatment will be the test as to whether or not the story has "legs."

An Interview with Jon Sherman, Supervising Producer, Frasier

On story day we gather around the table and everyone throws out ideas. They may come from episodes we've already done or character attributes or simply something that's happened to someone. Often we draw on personal experiences.

Everyone chips in. When we hit a notion that seems as if it's the beginning for a story we begin to flesh it out. At this time, a writer may not be assigned to the story. If you feel the story resonates with you, you may step up and say: "I'd like to write this one." Nine times out of ten the executive producer assigns a writer to the episode. However, if it's an idea that you brought in and believe it could be a fun show, then you would get the right of first refusal or the first opportunity to write it.

As soon as we have something that moves forward, a writer gets the assignment. That's when we go to the board and start writing down things such as "Scene A, Frasier's Living Room" and the outline of a scene. A writer's assistant takes notes along with the notes on the board. And the writer who has the assignment also takes notes. So three sets of notes exist.

Quite a few ideas are thrown in and discarded even when they're put up on the board or find their way into the written transcript of the meeting. The writer's assistant will sift through the material and provide only those notes that work in the outline and the script. Those notes are put into scene order, and you have a rough outline of the scenes and the beats in the scenes and a little dialogue, because invariably people will pitch jokes and that keeps the momentum going.

109

We call what we do an outline — about ten or fifteen pages. It's written on the right hand side of the page (see page 115) so when we bring it back to the staff everyone can make notes and suggest ideas on the pages.

In that outline you take what everyone agreed to and sharpen it by adding jokes of your own and amplifying it. When someone sits down and reads the outline they get an even better sense of the story, how it flows, including jokes along the way. The outline helps to make sure you don't have a story problem when you get to script.

If you have a strong outline then writing the script is pure fun. It's a lot easier to write the script than to write the outline. The outline is the design phase where you make sure everything builds correctly. For example, you figure out the act break where we go to commercial and where we're going to want to come back. You're also looking for jokes. There are times when the outline helps you see that a scene isn't funny. It allows you to look at each scene and make sure that everything adds up to a complete show.

An Interview with Al Rabin, former producer of the daytime serial Days of Our Lives

Head Writers are the most important elements in developing daytime serials. They, or their staffs, write the "bible." Generally that represents the first year of the show. It breaks down all the characters and their backstories so that when we join them we know where they come from. Those backstories may become part of the ongoing series as it moves forward.

After the bible is written we may have to throw some of it out because we start casting and putting life into the characters. Things begin to change very drastically.

Once we have a bible we prepare daily outlines in weekly blocks. Outlines for an hour show can run anywhere from eight to twenty-two pages. The Outline Writer in conjunction with the Head Writer maps out what happens on a particular episode. Generally you start with a Monday recap and a Tuesday through Thursday build and then a Friday hook to bring the viewer back. With detailed outlines, we don't have to read the dialogue because the Dialogue Writer must follow act by act, scene by scene what the outline tells them. The treatment or the outline is extremely important because that's the show from day to day.

Producers and/or networks respond to the outline and give notes. Agreement on the notes must come on the same day. Decisions have to be made rapidly because the show airs daily. The volume is enormous. It's as if we make 260 movies a year over and over again.

Outlines go to Dialogue Writers who have seven working days to deliver completed scripts. The writing office staff receives the scripts and make sure the Dialogue Writer has done what the Outline asked them to do. Dialogue Writers not only read the five outlines for the week but also the dialogue of other writers.

Story Editors, who should be good creative detail persons, review the scripts. They have to be very careful about characters' dialogue because if they say the wrong things and they get on the air they could affect next week, next month, or six months down the road.

The typical writing staff for soap operas begins with the Head Writer or Head Writers. Underneath them you have perhaps five Outline Writers and each of them does one outline a week. Then there are five Dialogue Writers. Staffs can reach up to fifteen people.

The Head Writer is responsible for continuity of character and story development. However, there are also coordinators on the writing staff and on the production staff who mirror each other. They guarantee that stories don't go off track.

Writers also have to be aware of the actors' schedules on a series. They should know who will be available and who has gone on vacation or is doing a movie. Availability will determine if a character is in or out so there's no conflict.

Understanding character is everything in a soap opera. It's not longterm story or weekly story, but character. Philosophically, we take a very psychological approach to characters. At every level, whether it's the bible, the outline, or the dialogue phase, when we get the script we should know the psychological underpinnings of the characters. In that way the audience will have an investment in the characters. They cannot be observers. Writers need to write feelings of the characters in order for the viewer to recognize their inner emotions.

The outline becomes the backbone of every soap. That's where we have to decide what works and what doesn't work. Everything that happens is in the outline. That's where we find the forks in the road. It doesn't happen in the Long-Term Projection because that doesn't tell us what happens in week one or week two. Assuming we've established the characters correctly, the treatment determines the success or failure of the soap opera. The two most important elements in a successful continuing drama are story and storytellers. The rest is fluff.

APPENDIX II

SAMPLE TREATMENT

A SCENE FROM AN OUTLINE
FOR A SITCOM

FRASIER
"Hooping Crane"
Written by Jon Sherman

ACT ONE

A) <u>INT. FRASIER'S LIVING ROOM – DAY/DAY 1</u>

The doorbell rings and Frasier
answers the door to Roz.
He's surprised to see her so
soon after work. Roz explains
that just after he left a mes-
senger arrived with an envelope for him, so she figured
she'd drop it by. Frasier is
surprised by her thoughtful-
ness. Roz says it was really
no trouble at all, it was on
her way, she thought it might
be important... Frasier:
"Couldn't see inside when you
held it up to the light, could
you?" Roz: "Not a damn
thing."

Frasier opens the envelope to find a thank-you note from a caller. He says he used to suffer from triskaidekaphopia, but Frasier put him on the road to recovery, and in gratitude he's included four tickets to that night's Sonics game. "That's nice," says Roz. "Yes," says Frasier, "although I don't think he's conquered his fears just yet." "Why?" asks Roz.

Frasier (OFF TICKETS): "The game's against the 76ers – you do the math."

Frasier appreciates the man's gesture, but doesn't much care for basketball. Plus, with Daphne away at the health spa, he and Niles made plans for a good, old-fashioned boys' night out: "Dinner at Le Cigare Volante followed by the Northwest Chamber Music Society's performance of 'Vox Balaenae'." "Wow." says Roz, "you're really painting the town pink." Frasier offers her the tickets, but Roz has a date with a Frenchman she recently met. Frasier says

that's nice, perhaps she'll
learn another language. Roz
doubts it - they don't spend a
lot of time talking. Frasier
maligns her promiscuity as she
leaves and Martin enters.

Inspiration strikes, and
Frasier tells Martin he has a
surprise for him. Martin is
immediately wary - "Your surprises usually start with me
having to put on a clean shirt
and go downhill from there."
"Well last I heard, basketball
games didn't have a dress
code," says Frasier, handing
him the tickets. Martin is
stunned. He thought Frasier
had forgotten they were sup-
posed to go to a Sonics game.
"Of course I didn't forget,"
says Frasier, covering.
Martin: "Wait. This isn't
like the last time when you
said we'd go, then shanghaied
me into that retirement home
to meet that girl who worked
there, is it?"

The doorbell rings. Frasier
is cornered. No, says
Frasier, this isn't like the

last time, they're really
going. Martin beams as
Frasier opens the door to
Niles. Niles enters and suggests they get going so they
won't be late. Martin is surprised Niles is going. Niles
is surprised Martin is going.
They each raise an eyebrow at
Frasier, who ushers them out
the door. Frasier: "I think
right now we're all a little
surprised." [16]

---

[16] © 2001, Grub Street Prod. Reproduced by permission of Jon Sherman.

REFERENCED FILMS AND THEIR WRITERS

A CHRISTMAS CAROL (1908)
Screenplay uncredited
Story by Charles Dickens

A MIDSUMMER NIGHT'S DREAM (1935)
Screenplay by Charles Kenyon, Mary C. McCall Jr.
Play by William Shakespeare

AGE OF INNOCENCE, THE (1993)
Screenplay by Jay Cocks, Martin Scorsese
Novel by Edith Wharton

AMERICAN BEAUTY (1999)
Written by Alan Ball

BEING JOHN MALKOVICH (1999)
Written by Charlie Kaufman

BOWFINGER (1999)
Written by Steve Martin

CHOCOLAT (2000)
Screenplay by Robert Nelson Jacobs
Novel by Joanne Harris

CIDER HOUSE RULES, THE (1999)
Screenplay by John Irving from his novel

CLUELESS (1995)
Screenplay by Amy Heckerling
Novel by Jane Austen (*Emma*)

DAVID COPPERFIELD (1935)
Screenplay by Howard Estabrook, adaptation by Hugh Walpole
Novel by Charles Dickens

EAST IS EAST (1999)
Screenplay by Ayub Khan-Din from his play

EMMA (1996)
Screenplay by Douglas McGrath
Novel by Jane Austen

END OF THE AFFAIR, THE (1999)
Screenplay by Neil Jordan
Novel by Graham Greene

GREAT EXPECTATIONS (1934)
Screenplay by Gladys Unger
Novel by Charles Dickens

HAMLET (1912)
Screenplay uncredited
Play by William Shakespeare

HAMLET (1996)
Screenplay by Kenneth Branagh
Play by William Shakespeare

HARRY POTTER AND THE SORCERER'S STONE (2001)
Screenplay by Steven Kloves
Novel by J. K. Rowling

HENRY V (1989)
Screenplay by Kenneth Branagh
Play by William Shakespeare

HIGH SOCIETY (1956)
Screenplay by John Patrick
Play by Philip Barry (*The Philadelphia Story*)

LIFE IS BEAUTIFUL (1997)
Written by Vincenzo Cerami, Roberto Benigni

ON THE WATERFRONT (1954)
Written by Budd Schulberg

PERFECT STORM, THE (2000)
Screenplay by William D. Wittliff
Book by Sebastian Junger

PHILADELPHIA STORY, THE (1940)
Screenplay by Donald Ogden Stewart
Play by Philip Barry

RICHARD III (1955)
Screenplay by Laurence Olivier
Play by William Shakespeare

ROMEO AND JULIET (1968)
Screenplay by Franco Brusati, Maestro D'Amico,
Franco Zefferelli
Play by William Shakespeare

SCENT OF A WOMAN (1992)
Written by Bo Goldman

SENSE AND SENSIBILITY (1995)
Screenplay by Emma Thompson
Novel by Jane Austen

SHAKESPEARE IN LOVE (1998)
Written by Marc Norman, Tom Stoppard

SHADOW OF A VAMPIRE (2000)
Written by Stephen Katz

SILENCE OF THE LAMBS, THE (1991)
Screenplay by Ted Tally
Novel by Thomas Harris

TAO OF STEVE, THE (2000)
Written by Duncan North and
Greer Goodman & Jenniphr Goodman

USUAL SUSPECTS, THE (1995)
Written by Christopher McQuarrie

X-MEN (2000)
Screenplay by David Hayden
Story by Tom De Santo, Bryan Singer

REFERENCED TELEVISION PROGRAMS AND THEIR WRITERS AND CREATORS

ALLY McBEAL
Created by David E. Kelley

ANNE OF GREEN GABLES
Teleplay by Kevin Sullivan, Joe Wiesenfeld
Novel by Lucy Maud Montgomery

BUFFY THE VAMPIRE SLAYER
Created by Joss Whedon

CAPITOL
John Conboy, Executive Producer

DAYS OF OUR LIVES
Created by Betty Corday and Ted Corday

ER
Created by Michael Crichton

FALCON CREST
Created by Earl Hamner

FRASIER
Created by David Angell, Peter Casey, David Lee

LAW & ORDER
Created by Dick Wolf

LONE GUNMEN, THE
Created by Christopher Crowe

PRACTICE, THE
Created by David E. Kelly

SAMARITAN HOUSE
Written by Michael Halperin

STAR TREK: THE NEXT GENERATION
Created by Gene Roddenberry

WALKER, TEXAS RANGER
Created by Albert S. Ruddy, Leslie Greif, Paul Haggis, Christopher Canaan

THE WEST WING
Created by Aaron Sorkin

XENA: WARRIOR PRINCESS
Created by John Schulian, Robert Tapert

THE X-FILES
Created by Christopher Crowe

APPENDIX V

COPYRIGHT AND REGISTRATION

Before submitting a treatment, screenplay, or an original teleplay to anyone, either copyright or register the material (some writers do both) in order to establish the fact that you wrote the material and it was written at the time you say you did in the event you need proof.

COPYRIGHT

Copyright is done through the Library of Congress (LOC). You need to fill out Form PA that can be obtained from the Library, Washington, D.C. 20559-6000. Indicate that you are submitting an "unpublished text" and include a check or money order (no cash) for $30.00 made payable to the "Registrar of Copyrights" (fee effective through June 30, 2002). Mail it to:

> Library of Congress, Copyright Office
> 101 Independence Ave., S.E.
> Washington, D.C. 20559-6000

In several weeks you will receive a notice with a copyright number that your material has been registered officially.

You can also obtain the form online at *www.loc.gov/copyright/reg.html*. Click on "Short Form PA" (requires Adobe Acrobat, downloadable for free on site). Print out the form, fill it in, and send it with your manuscript and fee via mail to the Library of Congress at the address above.

WRITERS GUILD REGISTRATION

To register your material with the Writers Guild of America, send a copy to:

> Registration Dept., WGA
> 7000 W. Third St., Los Angeles, CA 90048

accompanied by a check or money order for $20.00 if not a Guild member or $10.00 if you are a Guild member. Within two or three weeks you will receive a registration receipt with a registration number.

In no event should you place the copyright number and notice or the registration number and notice on your screenplay. If you do, those who read it will recognize that the screenplay is not the work of a professional. In any event, in the United States when you sell your material the official copyright holder becomes the production company who, for some arcane reason, is designated the "author" of the material even when they still list you as the "writer."

APPENDIX VI

WHAT EVERY WRITER NEEDS TO KNOW [17]

Reprinted with permission of the Writers Guild of America, west, Inc.

Introduction

The Guild provides this checklist as a quick reference to some of the rights to which you may be entitled under the WGA Minimum Basic Agreement (better known as the "MBA"). It also contains other information beneficial to writers working on films under the Writers Guild's jurisdiction.

To ensure that you are able to take advantage of the many protections afforded by the MBA you must deal only with Guild signatory Companies. If you work for a non-signatory company, the Guild cannot guarantee you the protections afforded under the MBA. If you are a member of the Writers Guild you may not perform services for a company or sell literary material to a company which is not signatory to the MBA. Before accepting employment or selling literary material, we urge you to call the Guild's Signatories Department at (323) 782-4514, to ensure the relevant employing or purchasing Company is signatory. Do not rely on the fact that a company has produced other films, or that the company promises to become signatory, or that other companies with similar names are now signatory to the MBA.

Do not use this checklist as a substitute for the MBA as it is not

[17] Writers Guild of America, west, Inc. © 1998

intended to, and does not, alter the provisions of the MBA in any way. In the event anything herein contradicts the MBA, the MBA controls. The references listed after each provision refer either to the MBA or to the Long-Form Television Guidelines for Writers, Producers & Executives ["Guidelines"] or the Guild's Working Rules ["Working Rules"]. The word "Company" also refers to authorized representatives of the employing and/or purchasing Company.

Note: WGA jurisdiction includes all employment by a signatory Company for writing services, options/sales of literary material by "professional writers" to a signatory Company, and options/sales by writers the Company agrees to treat as "professional writers" as that term is defined in the MBA. Please call the Contracts Department at (323) 782-4501 if you have any questions.

Part I

Long-Form Television and Pilots

Know the Assignment

1. Before you are employed, you should clarify with the Company the writing services you are being hired to perform. The Company must tell you the number of "steps" and the amount of money you are to be paid for each step. (Article 13.B.7., Long-Form Television Guideline #1, Working Rule #4) For example, know up front if you will be asked to write a separate story, or if you will go directly to teleplay.

2. The Company may not ask you to perform any services payment

for which is contingent upon the acceptance or approval of the material. This is prohibited "speculative writing." (Article 20.B., Working Rule #14) For example, the producer may not say "Write up the story and, if I like it, I'll pay for it."

3. The Company must notify you of any writers writing previously, and/or of any other materials upon which the work is to be based. Also, the Company must notify you of any writers hired to write simultaneously with you and of any writers hired subsequent to you. (Article 18)

4. You should ensure that any source material referenced in your contract is owned by the Company at the time of the assignment, and that all writers' contracts properly identify and reference the same materials upon which the work is to be based. You must contact and notify any other writers assigned to work concurrently. (Working Rule #12)

5. The Company must specify in your contract the name(s) of the person(s) who may authorize you to write, and where and to whom to deliver material. You should not deliver literary material to anyone other than the person(s) named in your contract. (Article 13.B.9.)

6. The writer should meet simultaneously with the producer and the network to discuss notes, and network notes should be delivered to the writer and the producer at the same time. (Long-Form Television Guideline #2)

7. If you are employed when the director is assigned, the Company should arrange a meeting between you and the director. (Article 48)

Getting Paid

1. Do not commence writing without ensuring that the deal is in place. (Article 13.B.7.f.) Do not deliver materials to the Company if the deal is not clearly in place. For example, the deal is considered to be in place when all the essential deal points have been negotiated and agreed upon or when commencement monies have been paid.

2. Complete and deliver the I-9 form, W-4 form, Certificate of Authorship and any other forms required by the Company in accordance with the MBA and applicable laws. The Guild has found that many times a writer's paycheck is delayed because the Company has not received these forms from the writer. (Article 35)

The Company is required by law to establish your eligibility to work in the United States prior to the commencement of services (by use of an I-9 form), which must be signed and dated in the presence of an authorized representative. In the case of direct employment (as opposed to a loan-out), the Company must also receive a completed W-4 form. Services may be deemed not to have commenced until these forms are completed and filed for each employment. If you are requested to sign a Certificate of Authorship that must be notarized, you may have it notarized by any notary public. This service is also provided by the Guild for members.

3. Send a copy of your contract (and any amendments) to the Contracts Department of the Guild. This is your responsibility. (Working Rule #3b) Do not depend on your agent to do this. Review the contract to ensure it accurately reflects your understanding of the agreement. As the writer, you must be covered under the Company's Errors & Omissions policy. (Article 28)

4. The Company must pay commencement monies, at not less than WGA minimum, to you by the next regular payday in the week following the week in which you are instructed to commence. (Article 13.B.7.f.)

5. The Company must pay you not less than WGA minimum for each piece of literary material written at the Company's request, within 48 hours of delivery, but not more than 7 days following delivery. (Article 13.B.9.) Late payment of 1.5% per month for monies owed will accrue immediately thereafter. If the budget of the project changes, the Company must make adjustments, if necessary, to the compensation previously paid to you to bring that compensation up to no less than applicable MBA minimums. You or your agent may invoice the Company for such payments.

6. When the project is for a network (or other television service such as USA, UPN or TNT), the Company may not use the network's failure to reimburse it as an excuse for not paying for material delivered. If you have an overscale deal which provides for two sets of revisions and a polish, the producer may have been authorized by the network to request and receive payment from the network for a "producer's draft," without having to submit each draft to the network. (There are two different MBAs which the Company may sign; the rules in this area are slightly different in each. Please call the Contracts Department at 323/782-4501 if you have any questions.) In any event, payment may not be contingent on delivery of a draft to a network, or payment from the network.

7. You may not perform services at terms less favorable than the MBA (including performing uncompensated rewrites or polishes). (Article 9, Working Rule #6)

8. The Company must make pension contributions of 6% of compensation for employment services (and sales when combined with employment) to the Producer-Writers Guild Pension Plan, and health contributions of 6.25% of such compensation to the Writers Guild-Industry Health Fund. (Article 17) [NOTE: The Pension Plan and Health Fund are separate from the WGA. [Employer contributions are subject to change. Contact the Plan and Fund for current contribution rates] Requests for employer reporting forms and questions regarding the Plan and Fund should be directed to their offices at 818/846-1015 or 1015 North Hollywood Way, Burbank, CA 91505.]

9. The Company must pay you appropriate residuals as your film is released to various markets (free television, pay television, basic cable, videocassette, cd-rom, multimedia games, etc.). (Articles 15, 16, 51, 58 and 64)

Protect Your Creative Rights

1. If you sell or option an original teleplay, the Company must offer you the first rewrite of the teleplay, unless time constraints render that assignment impractical. (Ensure you do not "waive" this right in your contract.) (Article 16.B.3.h.)

2. If you sell an original teleplay or you are employed to write an original teleplay and the Company contemplates replacing you, the Company is required to arrange for you to meet with a creative executive or producer who has read the material to discuss the Company's view and give you a reasonable opportunity to discuss continuing to perform writing services on the project. (Article 16.B.3.h.)

3. The producer or a creative executive must consult with you regarding each set of revisions requested.

4. The name of each writer on the project must be included on the script cover page until writing credits are determined by the Guild. Once the Guild has made a final determination of writing credits, only the names of the credited writers shall appear on the cover page of the material. (Article 37) [See sample*]

5. The Company must submit a Notice of Tentative Writing Credits [see sample attached*] and a copy of the Final Shooting Script to all participating writers on the project and the Guild. Participating writers are writers who were employed to perform writing services or who sold material under WGA jurisdiction for the project. (Paragraph 11 of Television Schedule A) The Company must list on the Notice the names of all participating writers and propose the writing credit the Company in good faith believes to be an accurate credit. Each participating writer (or the WGA) may protest the proposed credit and request a credit arbitration within a limited period of time. [See "Credits Survival Guide" which is also available upon request from the Guild.] You should contact the Company if you want the Notice to be sent to a place other than that listed in your contract for receipt of notices (e.g., new agent, changed address, etc.).

6. As a participating writer you must be given an opportunity to view the director's cut of the film within 48 hours of the Company's viewing. If, in lieu of a viewing, the Company is provided with a videocassette copy of the cut, you must also receive a videocassette copy of the cut. (Article 48)

---

* See page 141.

7. The credited writer(s) should be included in all aspects of publicity and promotion including press kits, previews and premieres. (Television Schedule A, Article 48, Long-Form Television Guideline #3)

8. The Company must include the Guild-determined writing credit in all publicity and advertising where the director or producer is mentioned, with certain exceptions. (Television Schedule A)

Part II

Theatrical Motion Pictures

Know the Assignment

1. Before you are employed, you should clarify with the Company the writing services you are being hired to perform. The Company must tell you the number of "steps" and the amount of money you are to be paid for each step. (Article 13.A.3., Feature Film Guideline #1, Working Rule #4) For example, know up front if you will be asked to write a separate story, or if you will go directly to screenplay.

2. The Company may not ask you to perform any services payment for which is contingent upon acceptance, approval, financing, or any other event. This is prohibited "speculative writing." (Article 20.A., Working Rule #14) For example, the producer may not say "Write up the story and, if I like it, I'll pay for it."

3. The Company must notify you of any writers writing previously, and/or of any other materials upon which the work is to be based. Also, the Company must notify you of any writers hired to write

simultaneously with you. If you make a written request, the Company must notify you of any writers hired subsequent to you. (Article 18)

4. You should ensure that any source material referenced in your contract is owned by the Company at the time of the assignment, and that all writers' contracts properly identify and reference the same materials upon which the work is to be based. You must contact and notify any other writers assigned to work concurrently. (Working Rule #12)

5. The Company must specify in your contract the name(s) of the person(s) who may authorize you to write, and where and to whom to deliver material. You should not deliver literary material to anyone other than the person(s) named in your contract. (Article 13.A.14.)

6. The Company should provide you with clear notes concerning your literary material (preferably a single set), and, when possible, in advance of any meetings to discuss the notes. (Feature Film Guideline #2)

7. If you are employed when the director is assigned, the Company should arrange a meeting between you and the director. (Article 48)

Getting Paid

1. Do not commence writing without ensuring that the deal is in place. (Article 13.A.3.) Do not deliver materials to the Company if the deal is not clearly in place. For example, the deal is considered to be in place when all the essential deal points have been negotiated and agreed upon or when commencement monies have been paid.

2. Complete and deliver the I-9 form, W-4 form, Certificate of Authorship and any other forms required by the Company in accordance with the MBA and applicable laws. The Guild has found that many times a writer's paycheck is delayed because the Company has not received these forms from the writer. (Article 35)

The Company is required by law to establish your eligibility to work in the United States prior to the commencement of services (by use of an I-9 form), which must be signed and dated in the presence of an authorized representative. In the case of direct employment (as opposed to a loan-out), the Company must also receive a completed W-4 form. Services may be deemed not to have commenced until these forms are completed and filed for each employment. If you are requested to sign a Certificate of Authorship that must be notarized, you may have it notarized by any notary public. This service is also provided by the Guild for members.

3. Send a copy of your contract (and any amendments) to the Contracts Department of the Guild. This is your responsibility. (Working Rule #3b) Do not depend on your agent to do this. Review the contract to ensure it accurately reflects your understanding of the agreement. As the writer, you must be covered under the Company's Errors & Omissions policy. (Article 28)

4. The Company must pay commencement monies, at not less than WGA minimum, to you by the next regular payday in the week following the week in which you are instructed to commence. (Article 13.A.3.)

5. The Company must pay you not less than WGA minimum for each piece of literary material written at the Company's request, within 48 hours of delivery, but not more than 7 days following

delivery. (Article 13.A.14.) Late payment of 1.5% per month for monies owed will accrue immediately thereafter. If the budget of the project changes, the Company must make adjustments, if necessary, to the compensation previously paid to you to bring that compensation up to no less than applicable MBA minimums. You or your agent may invoice the Company for such payments.

6. You may not perform services at terms less favorable than the MBA (including performing uncompensated rewrites or polishes). (Article 9, Working Rule #6)

7. The Company must make pension contributions of 6% of compensation for employment services (and sales when combined with employment) to the Producer-Writers Guild Pension Plan, and health contributions of 6.25% [Employer contributions are subject to change. Contact the Plan and Fund for current contribution rates] of such compensation to the Writers Guild-Industry Health Fund. (Article 17) [NOTE: The Pension Plan and Health Fund are separate from the WGA. Requests for employer reporting forms and questions regarding the Plan and Fund should be directed to their offices at 818/846-1015 or 1015 North Hollywood Way, Burbank, CA 91505.]

8. The Company must pay you appropriate residuals as your film is released to various markets (free television, pay television, basic cable, videocassette, cd-rom, multimedia games, etc.). (Articles 15, 16, 51, 58 and 64)

Protect Your Creative Rights

1. If you sell or option an original screenplay the Company must offer you the first rewrite of the screenplay. (Ensure you do not

"waive" this right in your contract.) In addition, in the case of a sale of an original screenplay, if there is a "changed element" (e.g., a new director or star) within 3 years of the rewrite, and no other writer has been hired, the original writer shall have the right to perform one additional set of revisions. (Articles 16.A.3.c. and d.)

2. If you sell an original screenplay or you are employed to write an original screenplay and the Company contemplates replacing you, the Company is required to arrange for you to meet with a senior production executive who has read the material to discuss the Company's view and give you a reasonable opportunity to discuss continuing to perform writing services on the project. (Article 16.A.3.c.)

3. The name of each writer on the project must be included on the script cover page until writing credits are determined by the Guild. Once the Guild has made a final determination of writing credits, only the names of the credited writers shall appear on the cover page of the material. (Article 37) [See sample attached.]

4. The Company must submit a Notice of Tentative Writing Credits [see sample attached*] and a copy of the Final Shooting Script to all participating writers on the project and the Guild. Participating writers are writers who were employed to perform writing services or who sold material under WGA jurisdiction for the project. (Paragraph 11 of Theatrical Schedule A) The Company must list on the Notice the names of all participating writers and propose the writing credit the Company in good faith believes to be an accurate credit. Each participating writer (or the WGA) may protest the proposed credit and request a credit arbitration within a limited period of time. [See "Credits Survival Guide" which is available upon request from the Guild.] You should contact the Company if you want the Notice to be sent to

---

*See page 141.

a place other than that listed in your contract for receipt of notices (e.g., new agent, changed address, etc.).

5. As a participating writer you must be given an opportunity to view a cut of the film in sufficient time so that any editing suggestions made by you concerning the film, if approved, could be reasonably and effectively implemented. (Article 48)

6. The credited writer(s) should be included in all aspects of publicity and promotion including press kits, previews, premieres, film festivals and press junkets. (Theatrical Schedule A, Article 48, Feature Film Guideline #3)

7. The Company must include the Guild-determined writing credit in all publicity and advertising, and the Company shall submit all advertising and press kits to the Guild in advance of publication for review. (Theatrical Schedule A)

Contact Information

Writers Guild of America, west, Inc.
7000 West Third Street
Los Angeles, California 90048-4329

Agency (323) 782-4502
Claims (323) 782-4663
Contracts (323) 782-4501
Credits (323) 782-4528
Legal Services (323) 782-4521
Registration (323) 782-4500
Residuals (323) 782-4700
Signatories (323) 782-4514
Main Switchboard (323) 951-4000
Member Services (323) 782-4747

Writers Guild of America, East, Inc.
555 West 57th Street
New York, N.Y. 10019
(212) 767-7828

SAMPLE SCREENPLAY OR TELEPLAY TITLE PAGE

(Name of Project)

by
(Name of First Writer)

(Based on, if any)

Revisions by
(Names of Subsequent Writers,
in order of work performed)

Current revisions by
(Current Writer, date)

Name, address, & phone
of Company (if applicable)

APPENDIX VII

FINDING AN AGENT

Every writer asks the same question: After I finish my treatment or my screenplay, how do I get someone to read it?

You have three ways to have a treatment or screenplay read and eventually purchased.

One: Your favorite relative owns a studio and will do you a favor. That's the quick and easy way — however, those are pretty long odds.

Two: Submit your material through a friend or associate with connections to a production company. This method may prove very effective since the motion picture and television business operates on personal relationships. Therefore, it's important to network with writers, producers, directors, and others in the industry.

Three: Submit your treatment or screenplay to an agent. Agents understand the business and usually know the likes and dislikes of producers and production companies. Some agents will act as editors and make suggestions for revisions that will help sell your story. Each agency has its own submission policy.

For young people, interning with producers, production companies, or other entertainment entities provides entrée into a world where competition for every job from the mailroom on up is fierce.

If you are a student or a recent graduate of a university or college film school in a major city, you can always find an intern position through the school — usually unpaid — with an entertainment company. A willingness to work, along with a certain amount of assertiveness and tact, will create a sense that you have value.

Most important of all are contacts you make during your internship and in school. Some of the people with whom you interact will end up in positions to help you. Or you may be one of the lucky ones who can help others.

Once inside the door, make it known that you have creative ambitions. However, keep in mind your ideas do not mean a thing unless you execute them — when they exist on paper, ideas become reality. Be prepared to present those notions in the form of a well-written treatment. Let the word get out that not only are you a valuable addition to the staff, but you can also provide material for production. After all, stories and scripts represent the fuel that feeds the fire of revenue in entertainment.

In the event that you cannot intern, then finding agency representation is one avenue to success in motion pictures and television. The list that begins on page 147 provides you with information on agents willing to read unsolicited material from new writers.

Before approaching an agent, make a strategic phone call and talk to an agent who covers your area. Diligent research will uncover agents involved in features and television. Calling a specific agent may get you more information then a general call to the agency operator. After all, agents are no different than anyone else. Many of them want to help and certainly most agents are looking for the next breakout talent — and you may be the one.

An excellent source for names is the *HCD Agents and Managers* published by ifilm publishing. A new edition is published every six months, making it the most up-to-date directory in the business. It provides names, addresses, titles, and phone numbers. You can also go online to agency Web sites for general information about the organization.

The agent to whom you speak in all likelihood will request that you send your story or screenplay for review. Do not expect a speedy response. An agent's first responsibility is to his or her client list. In addition, the material you send will probably be given to a reader for **coverage**. Coverage means that someone hired by the agency will critique your story or screenplay and make a recommendation in writing to the agent as to whether or not representation should be considered.

Do not be discouraged by rejection. That's the nature of the entertainment business. If you believe in your story, persevere and eventually someone will sit up and take notice. You may not sell your story or screenplay, but if it's well written, professional, and has an air of originality, it will become your calling card for future work.

The following statements and list come from the official publications of the Writers Guild of America, west:

"The WGAw recommends that a writer initially telephone an agency or send a letter of inquiry, rather than submitting an unsolicited script. This letter should be concise, outlining relevant credentials and briefly describing the nature of the work.

"As a courtesy, most agents will return literary material if a self-addressed stamped envelope is included with the submission. However, agencies are under no obligation to return the submitted material, nor can the WGAw assist in the recovery of non-returned material.

"WGAw "No Fees" Policy: Guild policy prohibits an agency from appearing on this list if it charges reading fees or similar fees as a condition to read literary material. Such literary material includes but is not limited to screenplays, teleplays, telescripts, stories, treatments, bibles, formats, plot outlines, breakdowns, sketches, narration, non-commercial openings and closings, long form story projections and/or pilots--including all rewrites and polishes thereto. Please contact the Guild at (323) 782-4502 if you find that any of the listed agencies charge reading fees or similar fees for this type of literary material. The WGAw "No Fees" policy also applies to agencies that refer writers to entities which charge reading fees or similar fees. NOTE: Some agencies on this list charge reading fees or similar fees for other forms of literary material (e.g., novels or plays)."

CALIFORNIA

[*] A TOTAL ACTING EXPERIENCE
20501 VENTURA BLVD., #399
WOODLAND HILLS, CA 91364-2350

[P] ARTISTS AGENCY, THE
10000 SANTA MONICA BLVD., #305
LOS ANGELES, CA 90067
(310) 277-7779

ARTISTS GROUP, LTD., THE
10100 SANTA MONICA BLVD., #2490
LOS ANGELES, CA 90067
(310) 552-1100

[**] BECSEY, WISDOM, KALAJIAN
9200 SUNSET BLVD., #820
LOS ANGELES, CA 90069
(310) 550-0535

BENNETT AGENCY, THE
150 SOUTH BARRINGTON AVE., #1
LOS ANGELES, CA 90049
(310) 471-2251

[**] BOHRMAN AGENCY, THE
8899 BEVERLY BLVD., #811
LOS ANGELES, CA 90048
(310) 550-5444

[**,L,P] BRANDT COMPANY, THE
15159 GREENLEAF ST.
SHERMAN OAKS, CA 91403
(818) 783-7747

[P]BRODER/KURLAND/
WEBB/UFFNER
9242 BEVERLY BLVD., #200
BEVERLY HILLS, CA 90210
(310) 281-3400

[**,P] BROWN, BRUCE AGENCY
1033 GAYLEY AVE., #207
LOS ANGELES, CA 90024
(310) 208-1835

[**,L,P] BUCHWALD,
DON & ASSOCIATES
6500 WILSHIRE BLVD., #2200
LOS ANGELES, CA 90048
(310) 655-7400

CAREER ARTISTS
INTERNATIONAL
11030 VENTURA BLVD., #3
STUDIO CITY, CA 91604
(818) 980-1315

CATALYST LITERARY
& TALENT AGENCY
(818) 597-8335

[**] CAVALERI & ASSOCIATES
178 S. VICTORY BLVD., #205
BURBANK, CA 91502
(818) 955-9300

[**] CHASIN AGENCY, INC., THE
8899 BEVERLY BLVD., #716
LOS ANGELES, CA 90048
(310) 278-7505

147

CONTEMPORARY ARTISTS, LTD.
610 SANTA MONICA BLVD., #202
SANTA MONICA, CA 90401
(310) 395-1800

[**] COPPAGE COMPANY, THE
3500 WEST OLIVE, #1420
BURBANK, CA 91505
(818) 953-4163

[**] CORALIE JR.
THEATRICAL AGENCY
4789 VINELAND AVE., #100
NORTH HOLLYWOOD, CA 91602
(818) 766-9501

DAVID & DAVID AGENCY
7461 BEVERLY BLVD., #402
LOS ANGELES, CA 90036
(323) 634-7777

[L] DIVERSE TALENT GROUP, INC.
1875 CENTURY PARK EAST, #2250
LOS ANGELES, CA 90067
(310) 201-6565

[**,L] DOUROUX & CO.
815 MANHATTAN AVE., SUITE D
MANHATTAN BEACH, CA 90266
(310) 379-3435

[**,P] DYTMAN & ASSOCIATES
9200 SUNSET BLVD., #809
LOS ANGELES, CA 90069
310) 274-8844

[L] ELLECHANTE TALENT AGENCY
274 SPAZIER AVENUE
BURBANK, CA 91502
(818) 557-3025

[**, L, P] ENDEAVOR AGENCY
9701 WILSHIRE BLVD.
10TH FLOOR
BEVERLY HILLS, CA 90212
(310) 248-2000

EPSTEIN-WYCKOFF-CORSA-ROSS
& ASSOCIATES
280 SOUTH BEVERLY DR., #400
BEVERLY HILLS, CA 90212
(310) 278-7222

[L] ES AGENCY, THE
110 EAST D STREET, #B
BENICIA, CA 94510
(707) 748-7394

FAVORED ARTIST AGENCY
8811 BURTON WAY
LOS ANGELES, CA 90048
(310) 859-8556

[**,P] FIELD-CECH-MURPHY
AGENCY
12725 VENTURA BLVD., #D
STUDIO CITY, CA 91604
(818) 980-2001

FILM ARTISTS ASSOCIATES
13563 1/2 VENTURA BLVD.
2ND FLOOR
SHERMAN OAKS, CA 91423
(818) 386-9669

[L] FILM-THEATER ACTORS
EXCHANGE
390 28TH AVENUE, #3
SAN FRANCISCO, CA 94121
(415) 379-9308

[L] FREED, BARRY COMPANY, INC.
2040 AVENUE OF THE STARS, #400
LOS ANGELES, CA 90067
(310) 277-1260

[**,L,P] FRIES, ALICE AGENCY, LTD.
1927 VISTA DEL MAR AVE.
LOS ANGELES, CA 90068
(323) 464-1404

GAGE GROUP, INC., THE
9255 SUNSET BLVD., #515
LOS ANGELES, CA 90069
(310) 859-8777

[**] GARRICK, DALE
INTERNATIONAL
8831 SUNSET BLVD.
LOS ANGELES, CA 90069
(310) 657-2661

GEDDES AGENCY
8430 SANTA MONICA BLVD., #200
WEST HOLLYWOOD, CA 90069
(323) 848-2700

[L] GELFF, LAYA AGENCY
16133 VENTURA BLVD., #700
ENCINO, CA 91436
(818) 996-3100

[**] GERARD, PAUL TALENT
AGENCY
11712 MOORPARK ST., #112
STUDIO CITY, CA 91604
(818) 769-7015

[P] GERSH AGENCY, INC.
232 NORTH CANON DR., #201
BEVERLY HILLS, CA 90210
(310) 274-6611

[**,L] GORDON, MICHELLE &
ASSOCIATES
260 SOUTH BEVERLY DR., #308
BEVERLY HILLS, CA 90212
(310) 246-9930

[L] GUSAY, CHARLOTTE LITERARY
AGENT/ARTISTS REPRESENTATIVE
10532 BLYTHE AVE.
LOS ANGELES, CA 90064
(310) 559-0831

GROSSMAN, LARRY & ASSOCIATES
211 SOUTH BEVERLY DR., #206
BEVERLY HILLS, CA 90212
(310) 550-8127

[**,L] HAMILBURG, MITCHELL J.
AGENCY
8671 WILSHIRE BLVD., #500
BEVERLY HILLS, CA 90211
(310) 657-1501

[L] HART LITERARY MANAGEMENT
3541 OLIVE STREET
SANTA YNEZ, CA 93460
(805) 686-7912

[**] HENDERSON/HOGAN
AGENCY, INC.
247 SOUTH BEVERLY DR.
BEVERLY HILLS, CA 90212
(310) 274-7815

[*] HERMAN, RICHARD TALENT
AGENCY
124 LASKY DR., 2ND FLOOR
BEVERLY HILLS, CA 90212
(310) 550-8913

[**] HOHMAN, MAYBANK, LIEB
9229 SUNSET BLVD., #700
LOS ANGELES, CA 90069
(310) 274-4600

[**] HWA TALENT
REPRESENTATIVES, INC.
3500 WEST OLIVE AVE., #1400
BURBANK, CA 91505
(818) 972-4310

[**,P] INNOVATIVE ARTISTS
1505 TENTH STREET
SANTA MONICA, CA 90401
(310) 656-0400

[P] INTERNATIONAL CREATIVE
MGMT
8942 WILSHIRE BLVD.
BEVERLY HILLS, CA 90211
(310) 550-4000

[**] JOHNSON, SUSAN AGENCY
13321 VENTURA BLVD., #C-1
SHERMAN OAKS, CA 91423
(818) 986-2205

KALLEN, LESLIE B. AGENCY
15760 VENTURA BLVD., #700
ENCINO, CA 91436
(818) 906-2785

[**,P] KAPLAN-STAHLER-GUMER
AGENCY
8383 WILSHIRE BLVD., #923
BEVERLY HILLS, CA 90211
(323) 653-4483

KARG, MICHAEL & ASSOCIATES
1319 WELLESLEY AVE., #205
LOS ANGELES, CA 90025
(310) 205-0435

[**,L] KLANE, JON AGENCY
120 EL CAMINO DR., #112
BEVERLY HILLS, CA 90212
(310) 278-0178

[**,P] KOHNER, PAUL INC.
9300 WILSHIRE BLVD., #555
BEVERLY HILLS, CA 90212
(310) 550-1060

KOZLOV, CARY LITERARY
REPRESENTATION
11911 SAN VICENTE BLVD., #348
LOS ANGELES, CA 90049
(310) 843-2211

[**,P] LAKE, CANDACE AGENCY, INC.
9200 SUNSET BLVD., #820
LOS ANGELES, CA 90069
(310) 247-2115

[**,L] LARCHMONT LITERARY
AGENCY
444 NORTH LARCHMONT BLVD.
#200
LOS ANGELES, CA 90004
(323) 856-3070

[**]LENHOFF & LENHOFF
9200 SUNSET BLVD., #830
LOS ANGELES, CA 90069
(310) 550-3900

LENNY, JACK ASSOCIATES
9454 WILSHIRE BLVD., #600
BEVERLY HILLS, CA 90212
(310) 271-2174

LICHTMAN/SALNERS CO.
12216 MOORPARK STREET
STUDIO CITY, CA 91604
(818) 655-9898

LUKER, JANA TALENT AGENCY
1923 1/2 WESTWOOD BLVD., #3
LOS ANGELES, CA 90025
(310) 441-2822

LYNNE & REILLY AGENCY
10725 VANOWEN ST.
NORTH HOLLYWOOD, CA
91605-6402
(323) 850-1984

[P] MAJOR CLIENTS AGENCY
345 NORTH MAPLE DR., #395
BEVERLY HILLS, CA 90210
(310) 205-5000

MARIS AGENCY
17620 SHERMAN WAY #213
VAN NUYS, CA 91406
(818) 708-2493

[**] MARKWOOD COMPANY, THE
1813 VICTORY BLVD.
GLENDALE, CA 91201
(818) 401-3644

[L] MEDIA ARTISTS
GROUP/CAPITAL ARTISTS
6404 WILSHIRE BLVD., #950
LOS ANGELES, CA 90048
(323) 658-7434

[**,P] METROPOLITAN TALENT
AGENCY
4526 WILSHIRE BLVD.
LOS ANGELES, CA 90010
(323) 857-4500

[**] MILLER, STUART M. CO.
11684 VENTURA BLVD., #225
STUDIO CITY, CA 91604
(818) 506-6067

OMNIPOP, INC.
10700 VENTURA BLVD., 2ND FL
STUDIO CITY, CA 91604
(818) 980-9267

[**] ORANGE GROVE GROUP, INC.
12178 VENTURA BLVD., #205
STUDIO CITY, CA 91604
(818) 762-7498

ORIGINAL ARTISTS
9465 WILSHIRE BLVD., #840
BEVERLY HILLS, CA 90212
(310) 277-1251

[*] PANDA TALENT AGENCY
3721 HOEN AVE.
SANTA ROSA, CA 95405
(707) 576-0711

[P] PARADIGM
10100 SANTA MONICA BLVD., #2500
LOS ANGELES, CA 90067
(310) 277-4400

[**,P] PLESHETTE, LYNN LITERARY
AGENCY
2700 NORTH BEACHWOOD DR.
HOLLYWOOD, CA 90068
(323) 465-0428

[**,P] PREFERRED ARTISTS
16633 VENTURA BLVD., #1421
ENCINO, CA 91436
(818) 990-0305

[**,P] PREMINGER, JIM AGENCY
450 N. ROXBURY DR.,
PENTHOUSE 1050
BEVERLY HILLS, CA 90210
(310) 860-1116

PREMIER ARTISTS AGENCY
400 S. BEVERLY DR., #214
BEVERLY HILLS, CA 90212
(310) 284-4064

PRICE, FRED R. LITERARY AGENCY
14044 VENTURA BLVD., #201
SHERMAN OAKS, CA 91423
(818) 763-6365

[**] PRIVILEGE TALENT AGENCY
14542 VENTURA BLVD., #209
SHERMAN OAKS, CA 91403
(818) 386-2377

[**,P] QUILLCO AGENCY
3104 WEST CUMBERLAND CT.
WESTLAKE VILLAGE, CA 91362
(805) 495-8436

[**] RICHLAND AGENCY, THE
2828 DONALD DOUGLAS
LOOP NORTH
SANTA MONICA, CA 90405
(310) 571-1833

[L] ROBINS, MICHAEL D &
ASSOCIATES
23241 VENTURA BLVD., #300
WOODLAND HILLS, CA 91364
(818) 343-1755

[*] ROMANO, CINDY
MODELING & TALENT AGENCY
1555 S PALM CYN. DR., #D-102
PALM SPRINGS, CA 92264
(760) 323-3333

[**,P] ROTHMAN AGENCY
9465 WILSHIRE BLVD., #840
BEVERLY HILLS, CA 90212
(310) 247-9898

[**] SANFORD-GROSS
& ASSOCIATES
1015 GAYLEY AVE., #301
LOS ANGELES, CA 90024
(310) 208-2100

SARNOFF COMPANY, INC.
10 UNIVERSAL CITY PLAZA, #2000
UNIVERSAL CITY, CA 91608
(818) 754-3708

[**] SCAGNETTI, JACK
5118 VINELAND AVE., #102
NORTH HOLLYWOOD, CA 91601
(818) 762-3871

[**] SHAFER & ASSOCIATES
9000 SUNSET BLVD., #808
LOS ANGELES, CA 90069
(310) 888-1240

[P] SHAPIRA, DAVID & ASSOC., INC.
15821 VENTURA BLVD., #235
ENCINO, CA 91436
(818) 906-0322

[**,P] SHAPIRO-LICHTMAN, INC.
8827 BEVERLY BLVD.
LOS ANGELES, CA 90048
(310) 859-8877

[**] SHERMAN, KEN & ASSOCIATES
9507 SANTA MONICA BLVD., #212
BEVERLY HILLS, CA 90210
(310) 273-8840

SIEGEL, JEROME S. ASSOCIATES
1680 NORTH VINE ST., #617
HOLLYWOOD, CA 90028
(323) 466-0185

[**] SINDELL, RICHARD
& ASSOCIATES
8271 MELROSE AVE., #202
LOS ANGELES, CA 90046
(323) 653-5051

SMITH, GERALD K. & ASSOCIATES
(323) 849-5388

SMITH, SUSAN & ASSOCIATES
121 NORTH SAN VICENTE BLVD.
BEVERLY HILLS, CA 90211
(323) 852-4777

[**] SOLOWAY, GRANT, KOPALOFF
& ASSOCIATES
6399 WILSHIRE BLVD., #414
LOS ANGELES, CA 90048
(323) 782-1854

[L] SORICE, CAMILLE TALENT
AGENCY
13412 MOORPARK ST., #C
SHERMAN OAKS, CA 91423
(818) 995-1775

[*] STARLING, CARYN TALENT
AGENCY
4728 GREENBUSH AVE.
SHERMAN OAKS, CA 91423
(818) 986-8938

[L] STARS, THE AGENCY
23 GRANT AVENUE, 4TH FLOOR
SAN FRANCISCO, CA 94108
(415) 421-6272

STARWILL PRODUCTIONS
433 N. CAMDEN DR., 4TH FLOOR
BEVERLY HILLS, CA 90210
(323) 874-1239

[**] STEIN AGENCY, THE
5125 OAKDALE AVE.
WOODLAND HILLS, CA 91364
(818) 594-8990

[**] STONE MANNERS AGENCY
8436 W. 3RD STREET, #740
LOS ANGELES, CA 90048
(323) 655-1313

[**,L] SUMMIT TALENT
& LITERARY AGENCY
9454 WILSHIRE BLVD., #320
BEVERLY HILLS, CA 90212
(310) 205-9730

[L] TRIUMPH LITERARY AGENCY
3000 WEST OLYMPIC BLVD., #1362
SANTA MONICA, CA 90404
(310) 264-3959

[**] TURTLE AGENCY, THE
7720 B EL CAMINO REAL, #125
CARLSBAD, CA 92009
(760) 632-5857

[L] UNITED ARTISTS TALENT
AGENCY
14011 VENTURA BLVD., #213
SHERMAN OAKS, CA 91423
(818) 788-7305

[**,P] UNITED TALENT AGENCY
9560 WILSHIRE BLVD., 5TH FLOOR
BEVERLY HILLS, CA 90212
(310) 273-6700

[**,P] VISION ART MANAGEMENT
9200 SUNSET BLVD., PENTHOUSE 1
LOS ANGELES, CA 90069
(310) 888-3288

[**] WARDEN, WHITE
& ASSOCIATES
8444 WILSHIRE BLVD., 4TH FLOOR
BEVERLY HILLS, CA 90211
(323) 852-1028

[**, L] WARDLOW & ASSOCIATES
1501 MAIN STREET, #204
VENICE, CA 90291
(310) 452-1292

[**] WILSON, SHIRLEY
& ASSOCIATES
5410 WILSHIRE BLVD., #227
LOS ANGELES, CA 90036
(323) 857-6977

[**] WORKING ARTISTS TALENT
AGENCY
10914 RATHBURN AVE.
NORTHRIDGE, CA 91326
(818) 368-8222

[**] WRIGHT, MARION A AGENCY
4317 BLUEBELL AVE.
STUDIO CITY, CA 91604
(818) 766-7307

[P]WRITERS & ARTISTS AGENCY
(LA)
8383 WILSHIRE BLVD., #550
BEVERLY HILLS, CA 90211
(323) 866-0900

NEW YORK

[L] ABRAMS ARTISTS AGENCY
275 SEVENTH AVE, 26TH FL.
NEW YORK, NY 10001
(646) 486-4600

ADAMS, BRET LTD.
448 WEST 44TH ST.
NEW YORK, NY 10036
(212) 765-5630

[*] AMATO, MICHAEL AGENCY
1650 BROADWAY, SUITE 307
NEW YORK, NY 10019
(212) 247-4456

[**,P] AGENCY FOR
THE PERFORMING ARTS
888 7TH AVE.
NEW YORK, NY 10106
(212) 582-1500

[L] AMRON DEVELOPMENT, INC.
77 HORTON PL.
SYOSSET, NY 11791
(516) 364-0238

[L] AMSTERDAM, MARCIA AGENCY
41 WEST 82ND ST.
NEW YORK, NY 10024-5613
(212) 873-4945

ARTISTS AGENCY, INC.
230 WEST 55TH STREET, #29D
NEW YORK, NY 10019
(212) 245-6960

[L, **] BERMAN, BOALS
& FLYNN, INC.
208 WEST 30TH STREET, #401
NEW YORK, NY 10001
(212) 868-1068

[**] LILLIE BLAYZE AGENCY, INC.
3000 MARCUS AVE., #LL08
LAKE SUCCESS, NY 11042

[**] BORCHARDT, GEORGES INC.
136 EAST 57TH ST.
NEW YORK, NY 10022
(212) 753-5785

BROWN, CURTIS, LTD.
10 ASTOR PL.
NEW YORK, NY 10003
(212) 473-5400

[L] BROWNE, PEMA, LTD.
PINE RD, HCR BOX 104B
NEVERSINK, NY 12765
(914) 985-2936

[**] BUCHWALD, DON
& ASSOCIATES
10 EAST 44TH ST.
NEW YORK, NY 10017
(212) 867-1070

[**] CARASSO, JOSEPH MARTIN, ESQ.
305 BROADWAY, #1204
NEW YORK, NY 10007
(212) 732-0500

[L] CARRY-WILLIAMS AGENCY
49 WEST 46 STREET
NEW YORK, NY 10036
(212) 768-2793

CARVAINIS, MARIA AGENCY
1350 AVE OF THE AMERICAS, #2950
NEW YORK, NY 10019
(212) 245-6365

[L] DEE MURA ENTERPRISES, INC.
269 WEST SHORE DR.
MASSAPEQUA, NY 11758
(516) 795-1616

DONADIO & ASHWORTH, INC.
121 WEST 27TH ST.
NEW YORK, NY 10001
(212) 691-8077

[**] DUVA-FLACK ASSOCIATES, INC.
200 WEST 57TH STREET, #1008
NEW YORK, NY 10019
(212) 957-6000

[L,**] EARTH TRACKS ARTISTS
AGENCY
4809 AVE, NORTH, #286
BROOKLYN, NY 11234

[S] FREEDMAN, ROBERT A.
DRAMATIC AGENCY, INC.
1501 BROADWAY, #2310
NEW YORK, NY 10036
(212) 840-5760

GERSH AGENCY, INC., THE
130 WEST 42ND ST.
NEW YORK, NY 10036
(212) 997-1818

[**,L] GURMAN, SUSAN AGENCY
865 WEST END AVE., #15A
NEW YORK, NY 10025
(212) 749-4618

[L] HASHAGEN,
RICK & ASSOCIATES
157 WEST 57TH ST.
NEW YORK, NY 10019
(212) 315-3130

HOGENSON, BARBARA AGENCY,
INC.
165 WEST END AVE., #19-C
NEW YORK, NY 10023
(212) 874-8084

[*,L] HUDSON AGENCY
3 TRAVIS LN.
MONTROSE, NY 10548
(914) 737-1475

[P] INTERNATIONAL CREATIVE
MGMT
40 WEST 57TH ST.
NEW YORK, NY 10019
(212) 556-5600

[L] JANSON, MARILYN JUNE
LITERARY AGENCY
4 ALDER CT.
SELDEN, NY 11784
(516) 696-4661

[**] KALLIOPE ENTERPRISES, INC.
15 LARCH DR.
NEW HYDE, NY 11040
(516) 248-2963

[L,**] KERIN-GOLDBERG
ASSOCIATES, INC.
155 EAST 55TH ST.
NEW YORK, NY 10022
(212) 838-7373

[L] KETAY, JOYCE AGENCY, INC.
1501 BROADWAY, #1908
NEW YORK, NY 10036
(212) 354-6825

[L] KING, ARCHER, LTD.
244 WEST 54TH ST., 12TH FL.
NEW YORK, NY 10019
(212) 765-3103

[L] KINGDOM INDUSTRIES LTD.
118-11 195TH ST., P O BOX 310
SAINT ALBANS, NY 11412-0310
(718) 949-9804

[L] KMA AGENCY
11 BROADWAY, SUITE 1101
NEW YORK, NY 10004
(212) 581-4610

[*,L] KOZAK, OTTO
LITERARY & MOTION
PICTURE AGENCY
114 CORONADO STREET
ATLANTIC BEACH, NY 11509

[**] LASERSON CREATIVE
358 13TH ST.
BROOKLYN, NY 11215
(718) 832-1785

[*] LIONIZE, INC.
2020 BROADWAY, #2A
NEW YORK, NY 10023
(212) 579-5414

[L] LITERARY GROUP INT'L
270 LAFAYETTE ST., #1505
NEW YORK, NY 10012
(212) 274-1616

[**] LORD, STERLING
LITERISTIC, INC.
65 BLEECKER ST.
NEW YORK, NY 10012
(212) 780-6050

[**,L] LUEDTKE AGENCY, THE
1674 BROADWAY, #7A
NEW YORK, NY 10019
(212) 765-9564

MARKSON, ELAINE LITERARY
AGENCY
44 GREENWICH AVE.
NEW YORK, NY 10011
(212) 243-8480

[**] MATSON, HAROLD, CO., INC.
276 FIFTH AVE.
NEW YORK, NY 10001
(212) 679-4490

[L] MC INTOSH AND OTIS, INC.
353 LEXINGTON AVE.
NEW YORK, NY 10016
(212) 687-7400

MEYERS, ALLAN S. AGENCY
105 COURT ST.
BROOKLYN, NY 11201

MILESTONE LITERARY AGENCY
247 WEST 26TH ST., #3A
NEW YORK, NY 10001
(212) 691-0560

[P] MORRIS, WILLIAM AGENCY, INC.
1325 AVE OF THE AMERICAS
NEW YORK, NY 10019
(212) 586-5100

[L] MORRISON, HENRY, INC.
105 SOUTH BEDFORD RD., #306-A
MOUNT KISCO, NY 10549
(914) 666-3500

[**,L] OMNIBUS PRODUCTIONS
184 THOMPSON ST., #1-G
NEW YORK, NY 10012
(212) 995-2941

OMNIPOP, INC. TALENT AGENCY
55 WEST OLD COUNTRY RD.
HICKSVILLE, NY 11801
(516) 937-6011

[**]OSCARD, FIFI AGENCY, INC.
24 WEST 40TH ST., 17TH FLOOR
NEW YORK, NY 10018
(212) 764-1100

[**] PALMER, DOROTHY AGENCY
235 WEST 56TH ST., #24K
NEW YORK, NY 10019
(212) 765-4280

PARAMUSE ARTISTS ASSOCIATION
25 CENTRAL PARK WEST, #1B
NEW YORK, NY 10023
(212) 758-5055

[*,L] PEREGRINE WHITTLESEY
AGENCY
345 EAST 80TH STREET
NEW YORK, NY 10021
(212) 737-0153

[**] PROFESSIONAL ARTISTS
UNLTD.
321 WEST 44TH STREET, #605
NEW YORK, NY 10036
(212) 247-8770

[S] RAINES AND RAINES
71 PARK AVE.
NEW YORK, NY 10016
(212) 684-5160

[**] ROBBINS OFFICE, THE
405 PARK AVENUE, 9TH FLOOR
NEW YORK, NY 10022
(212) 223-0720

ROBERTS, FLORA, INC.
157 WEST 57TH ST.
NEW YORK, NY 10019
(212) 355-4165

[L] SANDERS, VICTORIA LITERARY
AGENCY
241 AVE OF THE AMERICAS
NEW YORK, NY 10014
(212) 633-8811

[*,L] SCHULMAN, SUSAN
LITERARY AGENCY
454 WEST 44TH ST.
NEW YORK, NY 10036
(212) 713-1633

[L] SCHWARTZ, LAURENS R., ESQ.
5 EAST 22ND ST., #15D
NEW YORK, NY 10010-5315

[**] SEIGEL, ROBERT L
67-21F 193RD LN.
FRESH MEADOWS, NY 11365
(718) 454-7044

[**] SELMAN, EDYTHEA GINIS
LITERARY AGENT
14 WASHINGTON PL.
NEW YORK, NY 10003
(212) 473-1874

[*,L] STEELE, LYLE & COMPANY,
LTD.
511 EAST 73RD., #7
NEW YORK, NY 10021
(212) 288-2981

STERN, MIRIAM, ESQ.
303 EAST 83RD ST.
NEW YORK, NY 10028
(212) 794-1289

[*]SYDRA TECHNIQUES
CORPORATION
481 8TH AVE., #E 24
NEW YORK, NY 10001
(212) 631-0009

[**] TALENT REPRESENTATIVES,
INC.
20 EAST 53RD ST.
NEW YORK, NY 10022
(212) 752-1835

[S] TARG, ROSLYN LITERARY
AGENCY
105 WEST 13TH ST.
NEW YORK, NY 10011
(212) 206-9390

WRIGHT, ANN REPRESENTATIVES
165 WEST 46TH ST., #1105
NEW YORK, NY 10036-2501
(212) 764-6770

[P] WRITERS & ARTISTS AGENCY
19 WEST 44TH ST., #1000
NEW YORK, NY 10036
(212) 391-1111

For agencies in other states log on to the WGA website, *www.wga.org*, and click on "agencies."

LEGEND

[*] This agency indicated it will consider new writers.

[**] This agency indicated it will consider writers ONLY as a result of references from persons known to it.

[P] A packaging agency is one that represents several people associated with a film or television project, rather than just one client. It receives a commission from the producer for the group of clients it represents rather than the usual 10% from the individual clients.

[S] Society of Authors Representatives signed through WGAE only.

[L] This agency indicated it will accept only a letter of inquiry.

If there are no symbols next to the agency, this agency will not accept unsolicited material.

AGENCY REPRESENTATION QUERY LETTER

Keep query letters brief and to the point. You should be able to tell your story in one or two sentences with enough punch to interest the reader in wanting to see the completed material.

No formula exists for the perfect letter. However, here are some points to consider:

- Single space your letter and keep it to one page.

- Address the agent by name. Do not use first names — familiarity with someone you do not know is inappropriate.

- Provide pertinent information about yourself. This is a chance to brag about your accomplishments, but make your comments short and breezy.

- Give the agent enough information to pique his or her interest, but not enough to criticize. This is the time to sell the concept. Save the details for later.

This letter is designed for new writers with no professional credits. It provides the agent with a good sense of the stories available. It informs the agent that this person has ambition and a possible future in motion pictures and television. Preparation by having one or two short films or videos is very important. Agents always look for writer-directors with talent.

SAMPLE LETTER – A

Ridley Writer
1010 Computer Dr.
Cyberspace, California 91000

[DATE]

Ben Tenpercenter
International Artists Conglomerate
555 Wilshire Blvd
Beverly Hills, CA 90000

Dear Mr. Tenpercenter:

I note that you and your agency consider material from new writers desiring representation.

I recently graduated from the University of Southern Concord. My produced credits include the following short films: writer-director of "Black Star" (winner of the Sundance and Austin Film Festivals for best live-action short), "Dustup," and "Ivy Climber."

I have completed a full-length screenplay entitled "Hell Breeds No Angels," along with a treatment for another film titled "The Ghost Walks."

"Hell Breeds No Angels" follows two young men and two young women on a gun-toting, robbery rampage across the country until their car breaks down in a small western mining community where they come to the aid of a desperate woman attempting to escape her tormentors.

In "The Ghost Walks," an alien from the fifth dimension becomes lost on Earth. Only one person can communicate with him, an autistic girl placed in an institution. After a hair-raising escape from a governmental organization intent on his destruction, the "Ghost" rescues the girl and brings her into the real world.

At your request I will forward both manuscripts for your review. Videos of my shorts are available for screening.

Thank you for your consideration.

Sincerely,

Ridley Writer

This letter comes from a professional writer searching for an agent. The letter gets right to the point by pitching the story in a dramatic and compelling manner.

SAMPLE LETTER –B

Sam Scribbler
1234 Screenplay Drive
Movietown, NY 10101

[DATE]

Ben Tenpercenter
International Artists Conglomerate
555 Wilshire Blvd
Beverly Hills, CA 90000

Dear Mr. Tenpercenter:

Two young women and two young men meet in Stockholm on their summer break from college and find themselves immersed in mystery, death, and romance.

Dark Angel has the dark overtones of a gothic romance including murder. The characters go through hell before they discover the truth about the events surrounding them. The story begins in light, goes through the torment of personal darkness, and finally evolves to a new kind of freedom.

As for my background: I was on staff at Universal and Fox; wrote numerous television series; wrote and produced pilots; write young adult novels; and currently have a play in production in Los Angeles.

At your request, I will forward *Dark Angel* for your review. I look forward to hearing from you.

Sincerely,

Sam Scribbler

APPENDIX VIII

FINDING A PRODUCER

Letters to producers are different animals. With agents, you want them to read the script and like it. But they don't produce and they don't put up money. They look for talent they can sell.

Producers search for projects that will interest actors and directors in attaching themselves to the screenplay and make it eminently saleable.

Your task is to get the story or screenplay to a producer in the first place. If you have no agent, or prefer to do your own spadework, the first step becomes a dynamic letter that sells the idea to the producer.

Writers who have representation should inform their agent that they are contacting producers. Some agents will prefer to do it for you. Other agents don't mind having the burden lifted off of them. In any event, always copy the letter to your agent so that you maintain a paper trail in the event of a dispute.

The most current, up-to-date list of producers can be found in *HCD Producers Directory* published by ifilm publishing.

This sample is based on an actual letter written to a producer. For copyright purposes, the story has been changed. However, as a result of a letter similar to this, a production company acquired the story.

SAMPLE LETTER TO PRODUCER

Stuart Scribe
1234 Penandink Dr.
Novel City, CA 90000
323-555-1000

(Date)

Marvin Mogul
Miracle Pictures
222 Alameda Ave.
North Hollywood, CA 90000

Dear Mr. Mogul:

In the late 1960s a young scientist convinced the Department of Defense that the next great weapon of war would be — THE PARAGLIDER!

Based on a true story, WINGS OF WIND follows a brilliant young paragliding enthusiast who runs away from his home on a ranch in Colorado when he's accused of a murder he didn't commit. Using forged documents and lying about his age, he wangles himself into NASA headquarters. He ends up at the Jet Propulsion Laboratory where he convinces authorities to let him test his theory.

He organizes the Paragliding Corps and the Defense Dept. orders him to prove his theory by taking the corps on a remarkable journey into the stratosphere and launching a battalion via paraglider into a war zone.

Over the course of his story, the young man falls in love, finds friends, enemies, and comrades but also grows up as the world enters the Space Age.

I believe this story has the heart, warmth, and adventure you look for in your productions. At your request I will forward the story of WINGS OF WIND for your review.

I look forward to hearing from you.

Sincerely,

Stuart Scribe

Not every letter written to a producer will end up in a sale. Many contingencies exist that have nothing to do with the merits of your material. It may be a genre in which the company has no interest. The company may have something similar in work and does not want to repeat itself. The story might have too high a budget or require special effects. Each element plays a part in the decision. With that caveat at hand, a letter to a producer makes its points clearly and with dramatic impact.

In the letter to Marvin Mogul, the opening line is a teaser — a caption designed to draw in the recipient. The next paragraph states unequivocally that this is based on a true story and since truth is stranger than fiction, it has high interest value. Then a very brief synopsis of the story lays out the basic elements along with the subtext concerning what happens to the story's main character as a result of going on his journey.

In summary, the three parts of a selling letter include:

- A high-concept caption line

- The body of the story with a brief description of the main character, a dynamic description of his or her problems, and the obstacles he or she faces

- The underlying theme of the story

SEMINARS WITH

MICHAEL HALPERIN

*For a dynamic, inspirational encounter,
arrange for a one- or two-day seminar with
Michael Halperin*
on
Character Development and Screenwriting

Michael Halperin also provides literary consulting services
to help you develop strong characters, insightful concepts,
and well-crafted stories that have impact.

Rates upon request

MICHAEL HALPERIN
206-283-2948
818.788.2725 (Fax)
e-mail: *michaelhalperin@sprintmail.com*

ABOUT THE AUTHOR

Photo by Alison Markinson

Michael Halperin has been called "the foremost authority on screen-writing in America." He has written for television, screen, and stage, and has published both fiction and non-fiction books.

He has worked as an Executive Story Consultant for 20th Century Fox Television and on staff with Universal Television. He has written and/or produced numerous television episodes, documentaries, and computer-based programs. Halperin wrote the bible and was Creative Consultant for one of the most successful syndicated animated television series, *Masters of the Universe*.

Halperin co-authored the award-winning, best-selling children's novel *Jacob's Rescue* and wrote *Writing the Second Act: Building Conflict and Tension in Your Film Script* and *Writing Great Characters: The Psychology of Character Development in Screenplays*, both of which have been adopted by universities throughout the country. His play, *The Spark of Reason*, was produced recently in Los Angeles.

He holds a BA degree in Communications from the University of Southern California and Ph.D. in Film Studies from The Union Institute, Cincinnati.

171

Writing the Second Act

Building Conflict and Tension in Your Film Script

Michael Halperin, Ph.D.

Every screenplay needs an attention-grabbing beginning and a satisfying ending, but those elements are nothing without a strong, well-crafted middle. The second act is where most of the action is: where your characters grow, change, and overcome the obstacles that will bring them to the resolution at the end of the story. Naturally, it's also the hardest act to write, and where most screenplays tend to lose momentum and focus. Author Halperin helps you slay the dragon with *Writing the Second Act*, designed especially for helping screenwriters through that crucial 60-page stretch. Structural elements and plot devices are discussed in detail, as well as how to keep the action moving and the characters evolving while keeping the audience completely absorbed in and entertained by your story.

MICHAEL HALPERIN is a professional writer whose numerous credits include TV shows (*Star Trek: The Next Generation*, *Quincy*), nonfiction books (*Writing Great Characters*), and interactive media programs (*Voyeur*). He has also worked extensively as a consultant in the television industry, including Executive Story Consultant for 20th Century Fox Television and Creative Consultant on the animated series *Masters of the Universe*. He currently teaches screenwriting at Loyola Marymount University in Los Angeles and is in the process of developing a business-to-business Web site for the entertainment industry.

$19.95, ISBN 0-941188-29-9
240 Pages, 6 x 9
Order # 49RLS

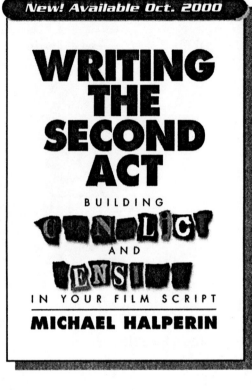

New! Available Oct. 2000

WRITING THE SECOND ACT

BUILDING

CONFLICT

AND

TENSION

IN YOUR FILM SCRIPT

MICHAEL HALPERIN

THE WRITER'S JOURNEY
2nd Edition
Mythic Structure for Writers

Christopher Vogler

See why this book has become an international best-seller and a true classic. First published in 1992, *The Writer's Journey* explores the powerful relationship between mythology and storytelling in a clear, concise style that's made it required reading for movie executives, screenwriters, scholars, and fans of pop culture all over the world.

Both fiction and nonfiction writers will discover a set of useful myth-inspired storytelling paradigms (i.e., "The Hero's Journey") and step-by-step guidelines to plot and character development. Based on the work of Joseph Campbell, *The Writer's Journey* is a must for all writers interested in further developing their craft.

The updated and revised 2nd Edition provides new insights, observations, and film refer[ences] on mythology's influence on stories, movies, an[d]

Christopher Vogler, a top Hollywood story con[sultant] has worked on such high-grossing feature film[s] Line and conducts writing workshops aroun[d]

$24.95
Order # 98RLS
ISBN: 0-941188-70-1